Getting Ready to Teach Reading for the New Teacher

Grade K

by

Anne Vander Woude

Published by Frank Schaffer Publications
an imprint of

McGraw Hill **Children's Publishing**

Author: Anne Vander Woude

Children's Publishing

Published by Frank Schaffer Publications
An imprint of McGraw-Hill Children's Publishing
Copyright © 2004 McGraw-Hill Children's Publishing

Send all inquiries to:
McGraw-Hill Children's Publishing
3195 Wilson Drive NW
Grand Rapids, Michigan 49544

Get Ready to Teach Reading for the New Teacher—grade K
ISBN: 0-7682-2920-0

1 2 3 4 5 6 7 8 9 MAL 09 08 07 06 05 04

The McGraw·Hill Companies

Table of Contents

© McGraw-Hill Children's Publishing   0-7682-2920-0 *Getting Ready to Teach Reading for the New Teacher*

Table of Contents

© McGraw-Hill Children's Publishing   0-7682-2920-0 *Getting Ready to Teach Reading for the New Teacher*

Reading Skills and Standards for Kindergarten

Phonemic Awareness

- blend sounds orally to make syllables or words
- give a rhyming word in response to a prompt
- identify the first and last sound of a word
- identify words that have same beginning (or ending) sound
- break a word into syllables

Phonics

- recognize and name alphabet letters, uppercase and lowercase
- identify the sound of each letter, including vowels
- identify beginning consonant sounds of words
- when shown a letter, give a word beginning with that sound
- understand basic vowel sounds
- begin to blend one-syllable words together (CVC—consonant, vowel, consonant, with a short vowel; e.g., c–a–t, cat)

Fluency

- can fill in words from a familiar story with repeated phrases
- can repeat a sentence or phrase after it is read aloud (echo reading)
- can say a familiar phrase out loud together with a group (choral reading)
- can say a familiar phrase with appropriate expression and intonation

Vocabulary

- describe a familiar object giving details about size, color, etc.
- identify words in basic categories (food, shapes, color)
- read one-syllable high-frequency sight words

Comprehension

- know that print conveys meaning
- can identify the cover and title page of a book
- create mental images from a story
- can make predictions based on pictures
- retell familiar stories
- ask and answer questions about a text
- distinguish fantasy and reality
- identify character, setting, events in a story

© McGraw-Hill Children's Publishing   0-7682-2920-0 *Getting Ready to Teach Reading for the New Teacher*

Introduction

How times have changed! The summer before I began to teach kindergarten, I went to our local public library to check out books on teaching kindergarten. The library had a grand total of two books, one of which was a book about Montessori kindergartens. There were no idea books, no blackline masters, no "how to set up the classroom" books, and definitely not a book on how to teach reading in kindergarten. We now have the luxury to pick and choose from among many wonderful materials. But where does a new teacher begin?

I hope you will find this book helpful. I wish I would have been able to find something like this all those years ago. A new teacher—whether new to the grade of kindergarten or new to teaching as a profession—needs practical, easy-to-use tips. And that is precisely what you will find here.

0-7682-2920-0 *Getting Ready to Teach Reading for the New Teacher*

Most of you will be given curriculum materials by your individual school or school district. A certain textbook or program will probably be required. You will be given lists of standards and benchmarks. (To find out how this book aligns to your state standards, go to www.MHstandards.com.) Even with all of this guidance, what a challenge to know where to begin! How do you know where to start and what is best for the children?

There are wonderful books about teaching literacy/reading at this grade level. However, you will probably not find time to read them during your first year in kindergarten. You will find a list of books I have found helpful in the resource list on page 138. Read some of them next summer!

This book can be used with any published reading series and any set of standards and benchmarks supplied by your school. My goal is to give you:

- lists of kindergarten reading skills
- several techniques to use in teaching the various skills
- easy-to-implement ideas
- hints on organization
- assessment and adaptation methods
- a resource list

- Read to the children often.
- Show them how much YOU enjoy reading.
- Read to them from a variety of genres.
- Talk about why you just LOVE the book you are reading.
- Read high-quality books.

The National Association for the Education of Young Children has many resources and position statements about developmentally appropriate practices. You can find references to them on the NAEYC Web site (www.naeyc.org). In this era of standardized testing, we kindergarten teachers must help parents and board members realize that not all teaching is immediately measurable and that not all children will learn the same things in the same month or year!

7

Implications

Reading instruction must be active and engaging. Try to include visual and auditory activities in almost every lesson. Use movement, manipulatives, music, chanting, writing, and so forth as often as possible. Teaching reading is one of the most important things a teacher will do. However, it cannot and should not be taught in isolation. It is only one subject in the curriculum.

Integrate reading into all subjects in your curriculum. Teach reading skills during science; teach science during reading instruction.

Since most kindergartners are not in school full time, a teacher often runs out of time! So reading must be taught in an integrated, multisensory, and altogether interesting and fun way! Let's get started!

Some Assumptions

- All children have unique ways of learning. They learn at different rates and in different styles.
- Children should be taught in developmentally appropriate ways.
- Reading is best taught across the curriculum. Integrate the teaching of reading within the other subjects.
- Reading is a complex act—readiness skills, physical factors, and social-emotional characteristics are all to be considered.
- Teachers must be good role models of reading!

0-7682-2920-0 *Getting Ready to Teach Reading for the New Teacher*

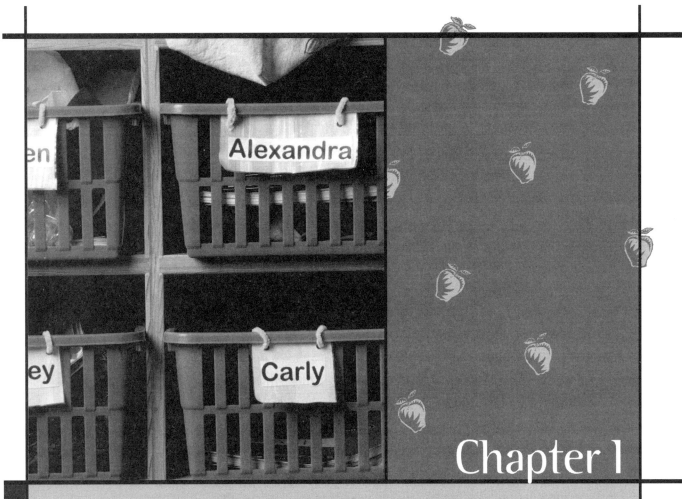

Chapter 1

Classroom Setup

In a kindergarten classroom, it is hard to separate literacy learning from all of the other types of learning that happen through the day. I believe that teaching across the curriculum is the best way to teach—partially for time considerations, but most of all, to meet the learning styles and developmental needs of the students. I am tempted, therefore, to include a sketch of an entire classroom, with its variety of learning centers. However, since this book is more narrow in focus, I will focus on those elements of the classroom that are used primarily to teach reading.

9

For Whole-Class Instruction

You will need to create a spot for children to do shared reading and writing together. This can be a special carpet or just a specific place in a carpeted room. It is usually the place the class gathers to do the daily calendar, have class meetings, sing together, or do other circle time activities.

COMMUNITY OF LEARNERS

I truly feel that reading is best taught in a classroom that becomes a community of learners. Building this sense of community must be done deliberately and involve the whole class. You foster this during the times of discussion, story reading, storytelling, showing and telling, when children are expected to listen respectfully as they get to know and appreciate their classmates. Each child frequently will be given the chance to show,  tell, give opinions, and make comments. While some children's academic skills will be more advanced than others, each child's developmental level must be valued. Even children who read fluently, for example, can benefit from practicing a–b–c songs with the whole group. It's fun, it's camaraderie, and it's working together. There will be other ways to meet individual academic needs—and several of these ways will be discussed later (see chapter 7).

It is scary for some children to risk trying to read in front of peers, or even in front of the teacher. An accepting and generous classroom community encourages children to take such risks.

Materials for Whole-Class Instruction

- big book easel and big books
- pocket chart
- sentence strips
- easel-size writing tablets
- pointers
- charts of poems, songs, etc.

Individual and Small-Group Work Area

Each child should have his or her own "seat" for individual work. Time is saved and instructions easier to give if each child knows where he/she will go to work. This is especially important when children are all working on the same activity. In my classroom, tables and chairs are grouped in the middle of the room; the learning centers are around the outside of the room. Classroom setups will vary greatly, however, and you need to find one that works best for you given the shape and size of your room.

Learning Centers

There will be many times when the children will be working independently in small groups in learning centers. These are times for the teacher to work with individual students on assessment screening (see chapter 6), pull aside a small group to work on various skills, or observe and learn about the students informally. The following centers relate both directly and indirectly to the reading process. (Many teachers more clever than I am come up with catchy names for these centers. Use your imagination!)

The procedures/rules for each center must be laid out clearly and understood by the children. These centers are intended to be used quite independently by the students. While some kindergarten teachers have classroom aides or make use of parent volunteers, you cannot be assured of that. I find it helpful to take a Polaroid or digital picture of the center when it is first set up and then display the photo near the center. This way the children can use the picture when cleaning up.

11

READING CORNER (Book Nook)

Set up an attractive classroom library with lots of quality children's books. For suggestions of titles to include, see the resource list beginning on page 137. You will need bookshelves or baskets to store the books. Try to get at least one authentic leveled bookcase so that some books can be displayed with covers facing out. You might want to make the area inviting with floor pillows, beanbags, or interesting chairs. I have seen teachers change the decor/theme seasonally or use such things as a small tent or old bathtub for the children to read in. I have found that floor pillows or beanbag chairs are great—inviting to the children, yet easily visible to the adult supervisor.

Tip For reading centers, some teachers prefer to have out just a few books at a time—up to twenty or so, and then change them frequently. I prefer to have many more than that available, so that I do NOT have to change them frequently. I find that by doing this, children often go back to find "old favorites." At times, I add stuffed animals for the children to "read" to. You could even match animals to certain books—a small mouse for *If You Give a Mouse a Cookie*, for example.

Start building your own collection of books now! Beginning teachers may not have lots of books of their own and probably cannot afford to purchase them. However, most schools have good libraries to use as a resource for classroom books. Other options:

▶ Use class newsletters to ask parents if they have any old, but gently used books to donate.

▶ Send home order forms from book clubs and then use bonus points to start your own collection.

▶ Use the public library to check out books. (Warning: Returning them on time is the problem for me!)

▶ Invite children bring a favorite book or two on a rotating basis.

© McGraw-Hill Children's Publishing 0-7682-2920-0 *Getting Ready to Teach Reading for the New Teacher*

In my classroom library, I have a "permanent" basket full of a-b-c books. I often add a basket of theme books—beginning school books in August and September, Valentine books in February, and so on. Be sure to include a good selection of other books including nonfiction books, poetry books, folktales, and historical books so children get used to seeing different genres. Don't neglect wordless books, emergent early readers, and "gimmick" books such as the "hide-and-seek" type. See resource list beginning on page 137.

WRITING CENTER

I recommend that this center be quite open-ended. It is an essential center, tying the reading and writing skills to one another. If you keep it open-ended, children of all developmental levels will benefit by writing in their own spelling. Here is where you can put materials for more advanced students later, if you wish. Simply set up a special writing folder for them to use. This should be done later in the year, after the children have formed a close community and they feel safe enough to risk at their own level.

The writing center should start out simply. I recommend having a stack of blank booklets made. A cover and about six to eight sheets stapled together works well. I always start the year with a book labeled "School Things." I find using half of an $8\frac{1}{2}$" x 11" paper works well.

The children look through school supply catalogs and cut out objects they use or would like to use in school. Then, they write the word on the page in their own spelling. They may also draw their own illustrations.

Sample covers for the "School Things" book and a few others are included on pages 108–110.

Materials for Writing Center

- scissors
- glue sticks
- markers
- colored pencils
- regular pencils
- crayons

Optional Items (and not all at once)

- gel pens
- scented markers
- gel crayons
- old magazines and school supply catalogs to cut up
- blank books with attractive covers
- stickers

Worth Investing In

- a set of stencils
- alphabet rubber stamps and stamp pads
- picture dictionaries

Changing subjects and magazines as the year progresses works well. Ask parents to save magazines and catalogs for you. (Be careful of clothing catalogs—the word *underwear* and pictures of it often send children into gales of hysterical laughter!)

If you want to change materials later in the year, you might add name cards for the children to use in practicing their names. Or, you could have the children stamp words with rubber stamps or use such things as rhyming stencils to make rhyming words booklets. I find, however, that by changing covers and writing tools occasionally, the children are satisfied with the same type of blank books throughout the year.

Tip Don't overwhelm yourself by trying to change materials too frequently! Children find it comfortable to repeat activities—they know what to expect and can gain confidence with familiar practice.

The writing center can be used as an informal assessment. Ask a child if you may save a booklet in his/her folder (more on assessment folders in chapter 6). Do this periodically for a good record of emergent writing. Some children will want the booklet back. In those cases, you could make a photocopy.

GAMES AND PUZZLES CENTER

Set up a center with a variety of games in it. Initially, a new teacher might not have enough alphabet and sounds games to make this center specifically for reading/phonics growth. Feel free to put general puzzles or board games of any kind here. The goal here is to have games with manipulatives, not paper work.

Materials for Games and Puzzles Center

- alphabet or consonant bingo
- letter concentration
- letter/sound matching games
- rhyming games

© McGraw-Hill Children's Publishing

Many games are available commercially at reasonable prices. You can make them, too, or have parents make them. There are books available for photocopying; many games can also be made on file folders. Parent volunteers could easily make these.

Games should be self-correcting and able to be used by the children independently. A game such as *Consonant Go Fish*, though very worthwhile, really requires adult help at first.

Some games can be made very quickly with index cards and stickers.

Matching Puzzles

Write a capital and small letter on each card. Or, cut apart the letters on the top of the alphabet cards on pages 130–136. Cut the two letters in half like puzzles, making each card slightly different. You can have two sets, alphabet a–m and n–z. You can use this technique for other skills, such as first-letter sounds or rhyming. Stickers are great as artwork.

The game is self-correcting.

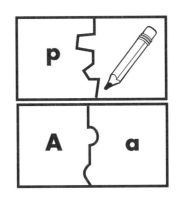

Memory

Using colored poster board (so pictures and writing don't show through) make sets of cards—ten to twelve pairs is plenty—and teach the children how to play memory with them. Again, you could use any readiness skill for this—capital small match, sounds and pictures, pictures and words, rhyming.

A-B-C Caterpillar

Cut index cards or poster board into twenty-eight small circles. Different colors make it more fun. Draw a face on one circle and a tail on another. Write one alphabet letter on each of the other circles. Mix them up. Have the children put the caterpillar together in a-b-c order.

© McGraw-Hill Children's Publishing

SMALL-MOTOR CENTER

My students find it humorous to think of their fingers as "small motors" that do a job. This center has materials in it which help the children work on their eye-hand coordination in a fun way. Many of the activities below use the pinching motion of thumb to index finger, which is so important in proper writing.

Lacing Cards

Materials needed:

▶ hole punches

▶ laces or yarn

▶ cardboard

▶ crayons or markers

Commercially made lacing card sets are fine, but children can also make their own. Have them draw a picture and then punch around the outside. They could use plastic laces or yarn for lacing.

Scissors Fun

Materials needed:

▶ various wavy or crinkle cut scissors

▶ paper

▶ glue sticks

▶ tape dispensers

Challenge the children to cut strips of construction paper and glue or tape them down on other paper. Using tape dispensers is a good way to use the pincer muscles, too.

Mazes

Materials needed:

▶ maze blacklines

▶ small stickers (incentive size)

Draw some very simple mazes. Seasonal ones are great! (See page 112 for sample.) Challenge the children to put small stickers inside the path of the maze.

See-Through Pictures

Materials needed:

▶ black construction paper

▶ large tacks

▶ spring clothespins or paper clips (to clip papers together while working)

Draw simple shapes or objects on a blackline—use dots instead of solid lines. The children put a black paper under the drawing and clip papers together with clothespin or paper clip. They poke holes with the tack. When finished, they hold the black page up to the light and the picture shows through. Some suggestions for pictures: circle, square, triangle, rectangle, diamond, oval, star, heart, apple, pine tree, leaf. (See page 113 for an acorn pattern.)

Modeling Clay

Materials needed:

▶ modeling clay (one color is fine)

▶ toothpicks or craft sticks

Show the children how to make snakes out of the modeling clay. In this center, they use snakes to make letters and words. Many children love to make their names with clay. You could also let them make a letter with a "snake" and an object to match, such as a "c" and a caterpillar. Another clay activity is pancake writing. The children make a pancake out of clay and then use toothpicks or craft sticks to write letters on their pancake.

Dot-to-Dots

Get a book of blackline masters with a–b–c dot-to-dots. Children complete them by carefully going through each dot. I often give them something special to color the picture with, such as rainbow crayons or gel writers.

OTHER CENTERS

New teachers might not have the resources and/or time to set up the following centers initially. Work toward having these two available later in the year.

Listening Center

Materials needed:

▶ sets of earphones and tape recorder with headphone jack

▶ multiple copies of books with tapes

Most school libraries have book sets like these. They are also available for good prices through book clubs.

Alphabet Crafts

In this center, the children make an object that represents a letter and sound. See the section on a-b-c crafts (pages 23–27) for suggestions.

Getting the Centers Started

As you introduce each center, remember to model every step involved, including the clean-up. You will introduce only one or two of these centers each day. It will be a couple of weeks before you have everything operating smoothly.

Center Rotation and Record-Keeping

Most beginning teachers find it easiest and most efficient to make a chart and assign children to the centers. This is also helpful to make sure that all the children visit all of the centers. While I prefer to assign the children randomly, it is possible to eventually group by skills. Sample charts are shown on page 19.

SUGGESTION 1

Randomly (at first) group the children into five groups. A color can be assigned to each group. Write student names on the appropriate color card. Hang each card at the center and the children will be able to find their work area.

DATE	BLUE	YELLOW	GREEN	PURPLE	RED
	Writing	Small Motor	Games	Clay	Dot-to-Dots
	Dot-to-Dots	Writing	Small Motor	Games	Clay
	Clay	Dot-to-Dots	Writing	Small Motor	Games
	Games	Clay	Dot-to-Dots	Writing	Small Motor
	Small Motor	Games	Clay	Dot-to-Dots	Writing

SUGGESTION 2

Some teachers prefer to let children choose where they work as often as possible. This seems to fit the teaching style or learning styles of some classrooms. You could keep track of this system by making each child a ticket and then punching or marking the date on the center each child chooses. Try to have children take turns being "first" choice. A sample ticket is below.

NAME	WRITING	SMALL MOTOR
Jordan	9/7, 9/20	9/8, 9/10
DOT TO DOT	**CLAY**	**GAMES**
9/18, 9/23	9/21, 9/13	9/15

0-7682-2920-0 *Getting Ready to Teach Reading for the New Teacher*

New teachers have so much to do and everything is new. You might or might not have many resources or ways to get them. Most kindergarten rooms, however, have at least some materials available: sand and water tables, art easels, housekeeping corner, jigsaw puzzles, big blocks. Don't be reluctant to use those centers for small groups of children while you are working with other groups or individuals. You can even take the opportunity to add reading activities to some of the centers. For instance, encourage the children to make a shopping list while playing house. Ask if they would like you to print a sentence or title to label their paintings. Give them a task card that says, "What can you make with twenty big blocks?" These are simple, quick ways to use what is already at hand in most kindergarten classrooms.

Tip Not every center must be labeled a literacy center for literacy skills to develop there! Language development, following directions, generating ideas, and talking to others are all parts of becoming a good reader and these skills are being practiced by the children while they work/play in many different kinds of centers, including art or play areas.

Now, get ready to "center" your reading instruction!

0-7682-2920-0 *Getting Ready to Teach Reading for the New Teacher*

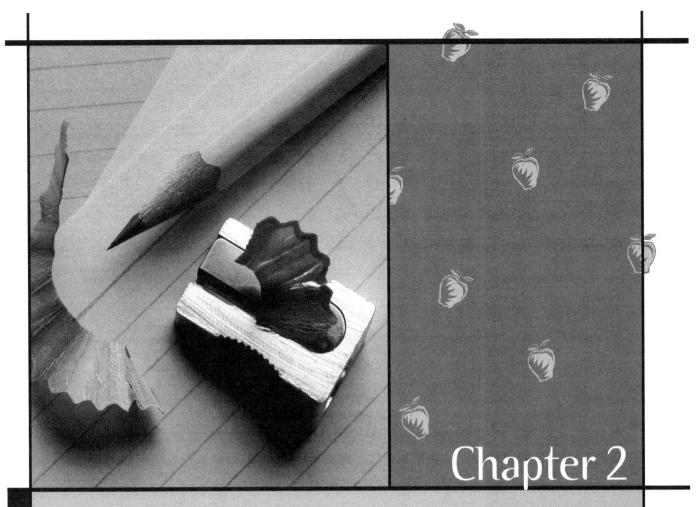

Chapter 2

Planning a Year's Curriculum

I know that science is best learned in the context of real-life experiences for the children. Math is best learned in the same context and so is social studies. What about reading? Of course, it is also best learned in the context of real-life experiences! But so often, because a school system has given a teacher a required text, the reading instruction becomes isolated from the rest of the curriculum. This chapter presents a plan to help you make your reading curriculum integrated, developmentally appropriate, and time-effective.

21

0-7682-2920-0 *Getting Ready to Teach Reading for the New Teacher*

I believe that the best reading program is one the teacher takes ownership of to meet the needs of his/her class. Look at your standards and benchmarks for reading and keep them in mind when designing the year's activities. Be systematic about it! Being creative and flexible does not mean being haphazard. The following approach is the one I have found works best for me. It is a theme-based curriculum. You will need to vary it depending on the units you must teach, the part of the country you are from, and the makeup of your school constituency, but the overall approach is quite adaptable.

Letter of Emphasis: A Systematic, Teacher-Designed Approach

Choose your letter based on a seasonal theme or take it from your science/social studies curriculum. All of the activities below are done during the course of our emphasis on the letter—usually a week. Notice all of the opportunities to fit in phonemic awareness, rhyming, and other skills.

PROCEDURE

Each letter is introduced with a song to the tune of "Skip to My Lou." You can make your own words for each letter or use the ideas given on pages 23–27. For example, for the letter s:

Summer sunshine, s, s, s, (repeat 3x)
Skip to my Lou, my darling.
(*Note: You sing the *sound*, not the letter name.)

Introduce each letter with a songbook. I make a large book with one letter per page to use with the class. The pages are not in alphabetical order, but in the order the letters are emphasized. Later in the year, when all of the letters have been covered, we take the book apart, and put it in alphabetical order together. Sample pages are shown in the sidebar.

SUMMER SUNSHINE

"s, s, s"

Skip to my Lou,
my darling.

BUMPY BUSES

"b, b, b"

Skip to my Lou,
my darling.

22

A-B-C CRAFTS

At the beginning of the school year, I teach each craft to the whole class as a group, as we begin to use scissors, glue sticks, crayons, markers, and other materials correctly. Almost every object is made with the "cut off the corners" technique. Each has a lowercase alphabet letter pasted on it. Later, these a-b-c crafts could become a center as mentioned earlier. Craft suggestions for each letter are included on the following pages. You can photocopy the top of the alphabet cards on pages 130–136 for students to paste the letter on each craft.

0-7682-2920-0 *Getting Ready to Teach Reading for the New Teacher*

Ee — "Elmer Elephant"

gray
2" x 6"

4" x 4"

3" x 3"
2

gray
6" x 6"

gray
1 ½ " x 2"

Ff — "friendly fire truck"

brads

2
3" x 3"
black

4 ½ " x 9" red

½ " x 9" yellow

white

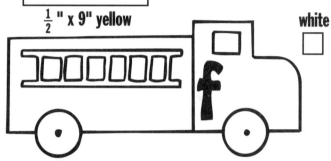

Gg — "garden growing"
(9" x 12" background any color)

3" x 12" brown

yellow/orange circles, scraps

3 ½ " x ½ "
green

2" x 3"

(several for each child)
fold stems so flowers
can "grow"

Hh — "holiday houses"

white
6" x 6"

2" x 3"
green

2" squares

9" x 6" red
to make roof

door opens

decorate with glitter or stickers

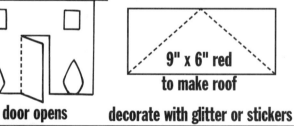

Ii — "Isaac Inchworm"

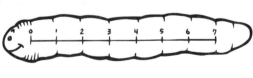

draw and
photocopy
using 7–8
inches

i

glue Isaac here →

things to measure →

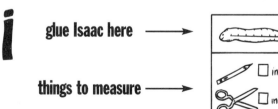
inches
inches

Jj — "jack-in-the-box"

4" x 4"

3" x 3"

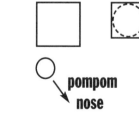

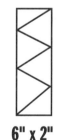

pompom
nose

6" x 2"
accordian fold

j

use any
contrasting
colors

3"

0-7682-2920-0 *Getting Ready to Teach Reading for the New Teacher*

Kk — "kites, kites"

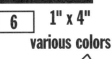

6 | 1" x 4"
various colors

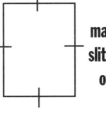

make four
slits ahead
of time

children make
a dot by each
slit, draw
lines, cut out

crepe
paper

Ll — "leaves are falling"

lots of small orange, yellow,
brown, red strips to tear

Students draw
tree or teacher
provides blackline.

Glue torn paper on tree, with
some "falling."

Mm — "monarch migrating"

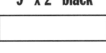
9" x 2" black

2" x ½"
black

Children draw black
lines on wings.

9" x 12"
orange
folded

Nn — "Nelly Nuttynose"
(Point out capitalization of names!)

9" x 12" background

nut

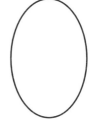

large oval for faces

Oo — "odd-looking ostrich"

4" x 3"
black

2 tan

beak

1" x 2"
tan
neck

5" x 4"
black

feet

feathers

12" x 6" background

Pp — "patch of pumpkins"

Kids draw vines.

3" x 3"

4
2-yellow
2-orange

4
green

brown or tan 9" x 12"

25

0-7682-2920-0 *Getting Ready to Teach Reading for the New Teacher*

Qq

"Queeny Quail"

3" x 4"

tan
6" x 6"

Kids draw legs and wings.
9" x 12"

brown or black
feathers

Rr

"rainbow, rainbow"

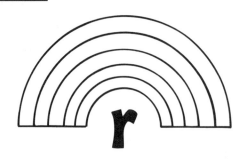

Draw blackline. Children color and
add stickers of multicultural children.

Ss

"summer sunshine"

yellow
6" x 6"

6   orange
1½ " x 4"

can also add sunglasses

Tt

"talking turkeys"
(paper bag puppet)

brown
6" x 6"

2 small orange triangle

red
3" x 6"

6 per child many
colors for feathers

wattle

bag
opening

glue "feathers" on back

yellow
2" x 3"

2

orange
1" x 4"

Uu

"ugly duckling"

gray

gray
3" x 2" - wing

bill

gray
6" x 4"

gray
4" x 4"

any color

— draw feet

9" x 12" light blue

Vv

"violet valentines"

Pre-cut dark and light valentine
shapes. Use lilac and purple. Kids
decorate with spangles, feathers,
tissue paper, etc.

Give one
away!

26

0-7682-2920-0 Getting Ready to Teach Reading for the New Teacher

 **"winter's coming"**

This one can be up to the teacher, depending on location. For "cold winter" people, snowflakes or snow people work well—or chalk on black paper.

fold
cut

white

 "fox and box end with X"

orange triangles

approx.

5" x 5"

any color

 "yardwork, yardwork"

Children draw yard in spring. Glue on fence pieces.

6 to 8 per child

"Zero the Hero"

A small zero can be made to circle each tenth school day on the number line. Draw a blackline. Kids make hat from scraps. Color on 100th day of school.

"Crunchy C" Casserole Recipe

1 cup cooked curly noodles
1 cup cooked chicken pieces
1 cup cooked carrots
1 cup corn (drained)
1 can cream of chicken soup

Combine in large pan. Cook.

Eat, using large corn chips

as spoons.

0-7682-2920-0 *Getting Ready to Teach Reading for the New Teacher*

PENMANSHIP

Another way to focus on the letter of emphasis is in learning to write. Work on the letter as in your own handwriting curriculum. Practice in the air, on each others' backs, on whiteboards, on a tray of sand—anyplace you can!

POEM

Reading poems is a great way to capture student attention (especially if they are silly!) and also to get students tuned in to rhythm and rhyme. *Read-to-Me Rhymes: Simple, Silly Poems for Every Letter* (Totline, 2002) is a great resource with several poems for each letter.

You can also write your own simple poems for students to make into mini-books. Poems with four short lines that feature simple objects would make fun books. For the letter *s*, for example:

| S is for **star.** | S is for **snake.** | S is for **sailboat** | on the lake. |

After reading the poem together, the children do tracking in their own booklets, going from left to right and circling each time they see the letter of emphasis.

BIG BOOK AND/OR POCKET CHART ACTIVITY

Big books such as *Sing a Song* (Wright Group) are another way to share the letter of emphasis. You can take any big book that you share as a class and pull out individual words that all begin with the same letter. Place these words in a pocket chart. If you use individual letters to make the words, you can pull out the letter of emphasis from each word.

 0-7682-2920-0 *Getting Ready to Teach Reading for the New Teacher*

CLASS DICTIONARY PAGE

The children are asked to bring one or two magazine pictures (early in the week) and they are glued into a class dictionary. Sometime later in the week, they watch as I write the words under each picture. If you have a big class, you will not be able to use all of the pictures. Consider assigning children on a rotating basis. Be prepared to find some of your own quickly in case children forget. This is one of those community-building activities as well as a time to model writing and review letters and sounds. Some of the more advanced children will be happy to suggest what letters to use! ("I'm writing the word *sun*. It starts with an *s*—what does it end with?")

A blank dictionary can be made by cutting white poster board into fourths, and using plastic bindings or loose leaf rings to hold it together. You can have a two-page spread for each letter to allow plenty of room to glue the pictures students bring in. One side of the spread has a capital letter, the other has lowercase. Decorate the cover of your class dictionary.

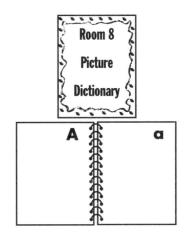

BOOKS

This is a time to read good books that emphasize the letter sound, too. Look for books that have many instances of the emphasized letter in them. For the letter *s*, for example, read *Sam's Sandwich* (David Pelham) or *Some Smug Slug* (Pamela Duncan Edwards). I put these special letter books in a basket in the classroom library for a while. (See pages 140–143 in the resource section for a list of books for each letter.)

SNACK

For the letter *s*, you could have square saltines. See the monthly theme chart below for other snack ideas for individual letters. *The Hungry Worm* song and book is available through the Learning Workshop. It's a fun way to have snack, but will not be tied in directly with the letter of emphasis.

© McGraw-Hill Children's Publishing   0-7682-2920-0 *Getting Ready to Teach Reading for the New Teacher*

Getting Started: An Overview

The following chart can be used to outline the year's curriculum and to mix the teaching of letters, sounds, phonemic awareness, and other reading skills in with your teaching of the other subjects. This chart is not meant to be all-inclusive; for example, the science themes are given, but not the objectives or activities. In the "Letter of Emphasis" section, the songbook theme is listed after each letter. (See pages 23–27 for more information about the song and crafts for each letter.) You are encouraged to add to this chart by adding a math column sometime!

AUGUST/SEPTEMBER

Other Integration

Song
- "There's a Spider on the Floor"

Snack
- square saltines

Books
- Sam's Sandwich
- The Wheels on the Bus

Big Book
- Sing a Song—Wright Group

Themes

School Rules and Monarch Butterfly
(life cycle and migration)

SCHOOL RULES
Letter of Emphasis Activities

- ▶ S—summer sunshine, song and object
- ▶ Safe at School—class-generated chart
- ▶ Bus Safety—booklet
- ▶ B—bumpy buses

MONARCH BUTTERFLY

Letter of Emphasis Activities

- ▶ C—caterpillar crawling
- ▶ M—monarch migrating

Other Integration

- ▶ Big Book: *Munch, Munch, Munch* (Wright Group), song and text
- ▶ Snacks: crunchy "C" casserole, bread and butter, munch muffins (make them in school?)

Recipe for "Crunchy C" Casserole

- 1 cup cooked curly noodles
- 1 cup cooked chicken pieces
- 1 cup cooked carrots
- 1 cup cooked corn (drained)
- 1 can cream of chicken soup

Combine above ingredients in large pan. Cook until warm. Eat, using large corn chips as spoons.

OCTOBER/NOVEMBER

Theme

Celebrating Fall with the Senses (discussions and activities in science related to the senses—focusing on trees, apples, leaves)

Letter of Emphasis Activities

- ▶ A—ants on apple (orchards, trees)
- ▶ F—friendly fire truck (fire safety week)
- ▶ G—garden growing (harvest)
- ▶ L—leaves are falling
- ▶ P—patch of pumpkins
- ▶ T—talking turkeys
- ▶ introduce "TH" digraph—Thanksgiving

Other Integration

Big Books
- Six Big Apples (CTP)
- How Apples Grow (Newbridge)

Books
- A Garden for a Groundhog (Lorna Balian)
- The Grouchy Ladybug (Eric Carle)

Rhyme Book
- Turkeys Everywhere (Totline)

Snacks
- apples, finger foods, goldfish crackers (graph), pumpkin seeds, tiny tacos

© McGraw-Hill Children's Publishing   0-7682-2920-0 *Getting Ready to Teach Reading for the New Teacher*

DECEMBER

Theme

Holidays (This has been left very general due to variations on the types of celebrations schools allow. Suggestions for letter themes might work for many!)

Letter of Emphasis Activities

▶ J—jack-in-the-box—to go along with a "Toy Shop" center

▶ W—winter's coming

▶ H—holiday houses

▶ D—decorated door

Other Integration

Book

- The Seasons of Arnold's Apple Tree (Gail Gibbons)

Snacks

- juice, waffles, holiday cookies, dominoes (white frosting piped on chocolate grahams to resemble dominoes)

Big Books

- A World of Homes
- A House for Me

JANUARY

Themes

Fun with Movement (how animals move, how people move), Pushes and Pulls, Gravity (A great resource is *Force & Motion K–2*, McGraw-Hill Children's Publishing with Fantastic Frogs™ Counters, Ideal School Supply.)

Letter of Emphasis Activities

▶ N—Nelly Nuttynose (walks) (For info on how to make Nelly, see page 25.)

▶ O—odd-looking ostrich (runs)

▶ I—Isaac Inchworm (crawls)

▶ Q—Queeny Quail (flies)

Other Integration

Big Book

- Gravity (Wright Group), also tie in nursery rhymes

Book

- Inch by Inch (Leo Lionni) Measuring activities in the animals theme. (How big is this stuffed inchworm?)

Black Inventors

- A booklet from Schooldays magazine. Near ML King Day?

Snack

- nibble mix (each child brings $\frac{1}{2}$ cup cereal, pretzels, etc.), omelets, insects (gummy ones), quiche (not correct sound, but quince jelly is hard to find!)

0-7682-2920-0 *Getting Ready to Teach Reading for the New Teacher*

FEBRUARY

Theme

Valentines, Friendship, 100th Day, President's Day

Letter of Emphasis Activities

▶ V—violet valentines

▶ Z—Zero the Hero (appears on our number line every ten school days)

▶ E—Elmer Elephant

▶ R—rainbow, rainbow
(Children color a rainbow and put multicultural stickers on it to represent the diversity among friends.)

Other Integration

Books
- The Velveteen Rabbit
- the Elmer series (David McKee)
- Rainbow Fish books (Marcus Pfister) (emphasis—how to treat friends; it's what's inside that counts)

Snacks
- vegetables, zebra cookies (white frosting piped on chocolate graham crackers)

MARCH

Theme

Busy Bodies (unit on body parts), Spring Is Coming

Letter of Emphasis Activities

▶ X—fox and box end with X

▶ K—kites, kites

▶ Y—yardwork, yardwork

▶ U—ugly duckling

Other Integration

Books
- The Skeleton Inside You (Philip Balestrino, shows X-rays)
- Yertle the Turtle (Dr. Seuss; his birthday is in March)
- A Great Day for Up (Dr. Seuss)

Big Book
- The King's Pudding (Joy Cowley)

Snacks
- "x's" (make pretzels into x's with a dab of "squirt" cheese), kabobs (fruit, cheese, bread cubes on toothpicks), yogurt, upside-down cake (make in class?)

33

Since all of the letters have now been emphasized, the "Letter of Emphasis Activities" column is changed to "Review Activities." Since the children's skills have been emerging and maturing, the review activities below are given as general suggestions. Know your class! This might be a good time to teach the color words and number words. Do many whole-group and small-group activities with pocket charts and big books. Work on concepts of print, sight words, segmenting and blending sounds, finding words in big books, and looking at emergent readers together. This is the time to put it all together!!!

APRIL/MAY/JUNE

Themes

Farms and Farm Animals (incubate eggs, research a farm animal, talk about crops and farm products and/or types of farms), Honeybees (buzzing hive) Review: Our Senses and Life Cycles (tie in to themes above)

REVIEW ACTIVITIES

Long vowels, if not covered earlier:

- A—apron
- E—eagle or Easter egg (if appropriate for your class)
- I—ice cream (dairy farm tie-in)
- O—oval (review shapes)
- U—unicorn or uniform

Digraphs:

- Wh—wheat farm
- Th—"Three Billy Goats Gruff"
- Sh—sheep
- Ch—chicks

Other Integration

Big Books

All books below are Wright Group books.

- The Farm Concert
- Mrs. Wishy Washy
- Wishy Washy Day
- The Little Yellow Chick

Folktale

- "Little Red Hen" (Find as many versions as possible. Compare and contrast. Integrate with art, music. Put on a play or make puppets?)

Nonfiction/Information Books

- Your library/media center can help you find very simple books about individual farm animals. (See "Research in Kindergarten?" on page 84 for ideas on how to do this.)

Chapter 3

Teaching the Skills

The standards and benchmarks for reading in kindergarten vary from state to state and from reading series to reading series. The differences are mostly in the phrasing of the objectives and the organization of the publication. Most agree on the kinds of skills to be taught, however. (See page 5 for a sample list.) Some curricula seem to assume that all children will achieve the same levels of skill by the end of the year. In the real-life classroom, this is not true. Some will learn to read fluently; others will make progress toward becoming emergent readers. Still others will be at a lower developmental stage. All of these are normal in a kindergarten classroom; all levels of development deserve our respect.

0-7682-2920-0 *Getting Ready to Teach Reading for the New Teacher*

This section of the book will:

- List and describe the skills to be taught.
- Give several examples of classroom activities.
- Refer to sources of further information and activities.

Assessment suggestions and resources will be covered later (see chapter 6).

This activity is also very effective (and more difficult) with a tape recording of familiar sounds. You could make your own, but that is very time-consuming. Two wonderful games with tapes you could use are Soundtracks and Animal Soundtracks, both by McGraw-Hill. They are intended for use with small groups or in a listening center. Use the tape first with the whole group; add the activity to your listening center later.

The skill areas covered in this section are common to almost all of the curricula. They are based on the National Institute for Literacy (NIFL) document called "Put Reading First." The entire document can be read online at the site below:

http://www.nifl.gov/partnershipforreading/publications/reading_first1.html

Phonemic/Phonological Awareness

Phonemic awareness is the awareness that our language is made up of sounds. These spoken sounds are put together to make words; they lead to comprehension. We give babies a very early informal training in phonemic awareness when we speak to them, read to them, and sing to them. Research is showing that a good sense of phonemic awareness is extremely important for a child to become a successful reader.

In kindergarten, there are many opportunities for informal phonemic awareness activities. However, teachers must deliberately plan for these lessons, too. (An added bonus: most of these lessons are fun and add to the community-building of the class.)

Most sources call phonemic awareness the ability to distinguish individual spoken sounds. Phonological awareness is hearing more than one sound and being able to manipulate these sounds with such things as rhyming, syllables and words, onset and rime, putting many sounds together, and taking the phonemes apart.

GETTING TUNED IN TO SOUNDS—*Guessing the Sound*

Put school items that make distinctive sounds in a large box with a cover. Such things as a tape dispenser, scissors, paper to crumple, paper punch, stapler, chalk and chalkboard, or a whistle will work. Ask the children to guess what's in the box. Then, tell them that they will have to guess by the sound of the object. Sit in a place where no one can see the object. Make the sound; the children guess what it is. Follow-up activity: Put the objects on display and let the children draw a favorite one.

0-7682-2920-0 *Getting Ready to Teach Reading for the New Teacher*

It's Noisy in Here!

There are actually many sounds heard in a classroom, even when it's not noisy. Have the children close their eyes and be quiet for about thirty seconds. After they open their eyes, make a list together of what they heard. Point out sounds that are outside the classroom, too. Read the list back to the children, stopping to listen specifically for each sound. Go outside and do it again!

> **Tip** Add some good children's literature. Old but classic books such as *The Noisy Book* and *The Quiet Noisy Book* (both by Margaret Wise Brown) are great. And don't forget *The Very Quiet Cricket* (Eric Carle).

Where's That Toy!

Bring in a toy that makes a fairly loud sound. It could be a music box, or some other electronic toy that makes an interesting (and sometimes annoying!) sound. Play the sound for the children. Choose two children to leave the room momentarily. The rest of the class decides where, out of sight, to hide the toy with the sound still playing. The two children come back and together try to locate the toy. Use different toys on different days. Get some with fairly soft sounds to make it more challenging.

Do As I Say!

Decide how many children you want to involve in this at one time. Tell them you will give them a job to do, but will say the directions just once. Start out with one thing, then add a series of things in subsequent times. Children will enjoy doing "silly" things.

Examples: Go and hug a chair; come back.

Get two pattern blocks; come back; put one on my head.

Crawl under a table; go around a chair; get a book; come back.

 0-7682-2920-0 *Getting Ready to Teach Reading for the New Teacher*

WORD PLAY WITH PHONEMES

The following are samples of phonemic awareness (PA) activities to help children recognize sounds, identify sound patterns, categorize sounds, and blend sounds. Remember PA activities are *oral*—no alphabet letters or written words allowed!

> **Tip** Consider using the actual word *phoneme* when talking with children. Tell them one sound is called a *phoneme*. It's not necessary to do this, but young children often feel big and special learning "grown-up" words.

First Sound Chant

This activity helps with identifying sounds. Chant the following:

Teacher: Tell me the first sound in *sun*.

Children: /s/ is the first sound in *sun*.

Teacher: Tell me the first sound in *bat*.

Children: /b/ is the first sound in *bat*.

(Be sure the children make the sound, not say the letter *s* or *b*.)

Later, when the children are more skilled at this, use a beat, snap your fingers, or tap your foot during the chant. The same technique can be used later on with ending sounds or middle sounds (difficult!).

Teacher: Tell me the last sound in *bed*.

Children: /d/ is the last sound in *bed*.

Teacher: Tell me the middle sound of *letter*.

Children: /t/ is the middle sound of *letter*.

 0-7682-2920-0 *Getting Ready to Teach Reading for the New Teacher*

Picture Poster

Divide the children into small groups. If they sit at tables, this is a good activity for the whole table to work on together. Give each group a large poster board and some magazines. Assign each group a picture. For example, one group gets a sun, another a picture of a goat, another group gets a fish, and another gets a monkey. Children work together to find pictures in magazines that have the same beginning sound (or ending sound) as the picture you gave them. They glue the pictures they find on the poster. Teacher should mingle and encourage while groups are working. After enough time has passed (probably about twenty minutes), the groups clean up and then explain their posters to the class. This could be an activity for one table group at a time during center time.

The Same Sound Song

This activity helps with categorizing sounds. The technique of making new lyrics to fit familiar songs (collected together in *Piggyback® Songs*—McGraw-Hill, Totline) works well with PA activities. You sometimes have to "stretch" the words a bit to fit the tune.

Tune: "Mary Had a Little Lamb"

Teacher: What's the same in these four words, these four words, these four words? What's the same in these four words: *bad, boy, box,* and *bump*?

Children: We know what's the same in them, same in them, same in them. We know what's the same in them. They all start with /b/.

Teacher: What's the same in these four words, these four words, these four words? What's the same in these four words: *cup, cat, cow,* and *cape*?

Children: We know what's the same in them, same in them, same in them. We know what's the same in them. They all start with /c/.

A great resource for songs (all divided by PA skills) is the Phonemic Awareness Songs & Rhymes series (Creative Teaching Press). There is an edition for fall, winter, and spring. Available on CD, too.

0-7682-2920-0 *Getting Ready to Teach Reading for the New Teacher*

Mix Them Up

This activity is useful for learning blending, a skill for later in the year. Get a mixing bowl and spoon or a real blender (broken is fine) for a prop. Talk about things you could blend: ice cream, milk, and chocolate to make a milk shake, for instance. Now say that you are going to blend something invisible to make real words—words to hear, not to see or eat.

Demonstrate dramatically:

"I am putting these into the blender: /c/ /a/ /t/.
I mix them up (pretend) and out comes _____."
(Children say "cat.")

You will have to model this process a few times. Make more words while interest lasts. Later, ask for a volunteer to put in sounds—have the child whisper them to you first.

The following skills usually develop for most children later in the school year. In fact, some standards and benchmarks charts list them as first-grade skills.

Segmenting

This is the opposite of blending. You could use the blending image again. "When I put milk, ice cream, and chocolate into the blender and make a milk shake, I can never take those things apart again! But, the neat thing about words is that I CAN take their sounds apart."

(Pretend) "I dump *cat* out of the blender and get / c/ /a/ /t/! Let's try some more!"

Deletion, Addition, and Substitution

Examples of deletion:

If I take the /s/ off *stake*, I get _____. (*take*)
If I take the /f/ off *flake*, I get _____. (*lake*)

Examples of addition:

What would I get if I put /er/ after the word *farm*?
What would I get if I put /ish/ after *self*?
What would I get if I put /s/ in front of *pare*?

0-7682-2920-0 *Getting Ready to Teach Reading for the New Teacher*

Example of substitution:

Some simple substitution can be done with kindergartners, especially beginning consonants. A familiar song like "Willaby, Wallaby, Woo" is a type of substitution. Examples such as below, however, are very difficult for most kindergartners.

Here's the word *pan*: change the /a/ to /i/ and you get _____.

(*pin*)

Here's the word *fish*: change the /sh/ to /t/ and you get _____.

(*fit*)

SYLLABLES

Listening for syllables is quite different from listening for individual phonemes. Don't confuse the children by working on syllables right after the above kinds of lessons.

Introduction

Tell the students: "Some words have lots of sounds and can be quite long. Some of them have more than one part. We call these parts *syllables*. Say it with me: 'syllables.'" Hold up an apple. "Say the word *apple*. Now, say it again slowly, /ap/ (take one bite of the apple), /ple/ (take a second bite of the apple). The word *apple* took two bites—it has two syllables!" Give each child an apple. Let them bite a few words: jun/gle (two bites), hos/pit/al (three bites).

Syllable Band

Pass out rhythm instruments. (You can use crafts sticks or even pencils if you have no rhythm instruments available.) Children repeat the words and tap the syllables at your signal: *butterfly* (three taps), *caterpillar* (four taps), *worm* (one tap). Let them suggest a few words of their own.

Clap Your Name

Have each child clap his/her first name in turn. You could make a tally graph for the most common number of syllables in a name.

© McGraw-Hill Children's Publishing   0-7682-2920-0 *Getting Ready to Teach Reading for the New Teacher*

RHYMING

Read Books with Rhymes

Rhyming PA activities at this level should always start with books that are full of rhymes. Nursery rhymes are considered an excellent preparation for rhyme recognition. There are several good books that are about rhyming. One is *A Bear Ate My Pear* (Kent Salisbury). Of course, books by Dr. Seuss and Bill Martin also come to mind!! Read many good-quality children's books with rhymes in them. Some newly developed emergent readers are a good source of rhymes, too.

Just reading books with rhymes, while essential, is not enough. Most children seem to grasp the rhyming concept when very young; some, however, have difficulty with identifying rhyming words and/or supplying rhyming words. Difficulty with rhyme may indicate the child will have difficulty with phonics skills.

Recite Rhymes Together

Use variations such as choral reading, reciting with a "beat" rap-style, or "cloze" techniques.

Example of cloze: There was a cat who wore a _____. (*hat*)

There was a cat who chased a _____. (*rat*)

Sing

Find rhyming songs to sing together. Especially effective are songs like "Down by the Bay."

Add Movement to Your Rhymes

Clap, stamp, or snap on the rhyming words. Give each child rhythm sticks or jingle bells to use on the rhyming words.

"Pack Your Suitcase" Game

You could bring in a small suitcase as a prop, but that's not necessary. Tell children you are going to pack your suitcase with words to go to Rhyming Land. Choose a word such as *man*. Think of rhyming words to go in the suitcase.

> In my suitcase is a *man*.
> In my suitcase is a *can*.
> In my suitcase is a *fan*.

If you don't want to just use nouns, you could use the phrase, "In my suitcase goes *tan*." In this game, you might consider *not* accepting "nonsense" rhymes. (For a related activity, see the "an" family worksheet on pages 127–128.)

Picture Rhymes

Find pictures of rhyming words. Use the pictures in various activities. This adds a visual element to PA, but since it still does not include words, I am using it here. Be sure you or the class says the picture names aloud with each activity.

▶ Match the pictures using a pocket chart.
▶ Make up a rhyme using two (or more) rhyming pictures.

> A Sound Way (Wright Group) is a good book with PA activities in it, including rhyming pictures you can photocopy and use.

Pantomimes

The actors are silent, but the audience is not! This activity is fun for partners. Model the activity with you being a partner, because you will need to think of two rhymes that are easy to act out.

▶ *cat/bat*—One person act like a cat. The other might pretend to pick up a baseball bat and hit a ball.
▶ *dog/frog*—Act these out with no sounds at first. If children can't guess, the actors can make the animal sounds.
▶ *king/ring*—One child might pretend to be putting on a crown, the other, putting on a ring.

Notice, you're helping the children use context to figure these out. This is an important strategy in decoding and reading comprehension.

© McGraw-Hill Children's Publishing   0-7682-2920-0 *Getting Ready to Teach Reading for the New Teacher*

Onset
the sound(s) before the first vowel in a word

Rime
the remaining part of a word

Onset and Rime

This is a skill that develops after the previously discussed skills are firm in the children's minds. At this level, you can expose the children to it during the course of other content lessons. Think integration of curriculum!

Examples:

▶ "A caterpillar cr—awls." (Children provide the word *crawls*.)
▶ "The monarch can fl—y." (*fly*)
▶ "It is the first day of f—all. Look at the l—eaves." (*fall, leaves*)

TIME FOR PHONEMIC AWARENESS

By now you should have a grasp on phonemic awareness and some practical activities to use with the children. But I know what you're wondering—how can I fit it all in, especially when teaching half-day kindergarten? Relax, take it a day at a time, and remember that many of these PA skills are implicit in the lessons you already teach. Add a few specifically planned lessons, and you're on your way! It will soon become a part of your teaching pattern.

Phonics

Phonics instruction is an important tool for kindergarten reading instruction. Phonics involves the written form of the language and the relationship of the sounds to the letters. Phonics instruction involves sound *and* sight, auditory *and* visual components. The following are sample phonics skills to be taught to kindergartners.

▶ Recognize and name alphabet letters, uppercase and lowercase.
▶ Identify the sound of the letter, including vowels.
▶ Identify beginning consonant sounds of words.
▶ When shown a letter, give a word beginning with that sound.
▶ Understand basic vowel sounds.
▶ Begin to blend one-syllable words together.
  (CVC—consonant, vowel, consonant, with a short vowel; e.g., c-a-t, *cat*)

Still need more?

Check out the following book, which is an actual PA curriculum.

Phonemic Awareness in Young Children—A Classroom Curriculum (Marilyn Jager Adams et.al., Paul H. Brooks Publishing Company).

What various sources don't agree on is whether all of these skills should be *mastered* in kindergarten. Here is the reality: children develop these skills at different rates and times and at their own developmental level. It is expected that each class will have a range of levels—that is normal! Not all children will read emergent books by the end of the year. It is important to respect this fact, while keeping your eyes open for a child with multiple areas of concern who should have early intervention of some kind.

Phonics instruction coexists with PA instruction. While the specific lessons aren't taught together, the PA skills help the children make sense of phonics. Research indicates that a systematic approach to teaching phonics is superior to an informal approach.

Phonics instruction at this level starts with learning alphabet letters and sounds. Since there are probably hundreds of idea books for teaching alphabet recognition, this section will contain only a few activities. It is assumed, however, that the teacher will teach systematically, whether using the text required by the school system or an integrated approach developed to fit in with the standards. Refer to chapter 2 and the "Letter of Emphasis" focus for details on an integrated approach.

ACTIVITIES TO TEACH LETTERS AND SOUNDS

▶ Repeat some PA activities, such as the "Pack Your Suitcase" game. This time, use pictures or word cards. "My suitcase must be filled with things starting with *Bb*."

▶ Make picture and word cards for the children to match. This can be a class activity on pocket chart or made into a self-correcting game in the games center. Word/picture sets are very versatile and can be used in so many activities: categorizing and sorting, patterning, etc.

▶ Practice writing the letter (penmanship).

▶ Read a poem (tracking activity to find the letter being taught).

▶ Make a class dictionary (see page 29). Students bring in magazine picture beginning with the same letter to create each page.

bug

cup

hat

45

▶ Present big books, pocket chart activity, or poster featuring a letter.

▶ Use snack to emphasize a particular letter.

▶ Read lots of children's books emphasizing the letter (see pages 140–143).

▶ Make sets of lowercase and uppercase cards for the children to match. These can be made in "attractive" game format or just on plain cards.

▶ A quick fun activity is to give half of the children lowercase letters and the rest matching uppercase letters. On the signal "Go," they display their cards and find their match without talking.

▶ Be on the alert for inexpensive card games available in many places, such as variety stores and supermarkets. Scholastic and Trumpet book clubs often have affordable phonics games.

▶ A quick drill activity is the "Box Four" method. This technique can be used for many skills. Have the children fold a piece of paper into four boxes. "Fold in half and in half again." Model and demonstrate the first time; this can be difficult for some children. "Open the paper, draw a line on the folds, and you have four boxes. Write *Bb* in one box. (Demonstrate). Write *Dd* in the next box. Write *Ff* in then next box. Write *Ll* in the last box. Now, make a picture of something beginning with the sound of each letter."

Later in the year, have children write the whole word of what they draw using their own invented spelling. Great for assessment.

Bb	Dd
Ff	Ll

An alphabet chart should be available to the children. It is best if the chart has the correct writing formation of the letter (according to the writing program you are using). Individual charts for children's use is helpful, especially since children's eyesight preferences for distance/close work will vary. Having this chart in front of them allows for quick reference when writing and thinking about letter sounds.

LEARNING TO BLEND (SOUND OUT) WORDS

CVC Words

Use mostly CVC words with three letters (or perhaps four letters if using digraphs or blends). This activity is appropriate only with a group that has a good knowledge of short-vowel sounds, or at least the short vowels of the words you use often. It could be an activity done mostly with small, more advanced groups while the others work in the reading centers. These children are ready to learn that a vowel between two consonants is usually a short one.

One of the best ways to do this is to make card sets of consonants and vowels. Say the sounds separately first, and then move the cards together as the children blend them to make the word. By putting up one word at a time, you will not need as many cards. If you leave words up in a pocket chart, you will need to have multiple copies of some letters, especially the vowels.

Word Families

This can be a good introduction to onset and rime. Make charts or use individual cards. Many children like to write/read these in houses! (See the "an" family activity on pages 127–128.)

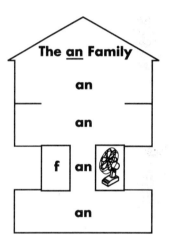

Vocabulary

While some phonics work is involved in the next section, most of the word knowledge involves vocabulary growth and sight words.

VOCABULARY GROWTH

When children know the meaning of many words, comprehension, fluency, and word-attack skills are improved. The following suggestions are ways to incorporate word learning in your classroom activities.

 0-7682-2920-0 *Getting Ready to Teach Reading for the New Teacher*

▶ Read many books with rich language. On occasion, ask about and explain word meanings.

▶ Have a word of the day or word of the week. Tie the word into the day's work. "Today's new word is *autumn*. It's another word for fall. Let's see if we can use it today."

▶ Make class lists of synonyms, referring to them as "words that mean the same thing." Synonym lists are especially effective when you are doing modeled writing on chart paper. It can often precede having the children write in their journals as you brainstorm a list of words together.

▶ Work with antonyms, using the word *opposite*.

▶ Add movement when possible, with or without written words. "I'll ask you to do something; listen closely. Do the opposite of 'clap loudly'. Do the opposite of 'open your mouth.'"

▶ Play "I can say . . ." to practice opposites.

Teacher: "I can say up,"

Children: ". . . and I can say down."

Teacher: "I can say smile,"

Children: ". . . and I can say frown."

▶ Work on adjectives, referring to them as "describing words." Fill-in-the-blank sentences on chart paper work well. "Today, we are going to make some sentences more interesting by adding describing words. It is a beautiful day. It is a beautiful, _____, _____ day." (Children suggest ways to fill in the blanks—warm, sunny, cold, snowy, etc.)

WORDS IN THE ENVIRONMENT

You can fill your room with many examples of words. I'm sure that many of you have bulletin board displays with lots of words on them already. Consider some of the following.

▶ Student's photographs labeled with names.

▶ Labels on classroom furniture, at centers, etc.

▶ Birthday graph with months of the year written on it and children's names on it.

▶ Message of the day or special messages: "Happy Birthday, Jim!"

0-7682-2920-0 *Getting Ready to Teach Reading for the New Teacher*

▶ Make poster-sized copies of your class-experience stories (places class has gone) or poems the class has memorized and display them where the children can read them.

▶ Put words the children use frequently on a word wall. If you have an alphabet chart displayed and have room under the beginning letter of the word, that is a great place to display the word(s). Model using the word wall when you do guided writing.

INTRODUCTION TO SIGHT WORDS

Sight words are those words that are used frequently and are often unphonetic. The children will not be able to just sound them out. Among the common sight words used by kindergartners are: *the, a, I, is, me, my, like*. Remember: it's simply a matter of exposure for most children, not a skill to be mastered in kindergarten. Use word cards and pictures, puzzles, coloring sheets, and other activities to help the children practice word recognition. (See the "Broken Hearts" activity on page 125 for a fun way to learn color words.)

Tip Teaching the children some "functional" sight words can be helpful for them when following directions on worksheets or in games. For that reason, teaching the color words and numbers words is a good option in your classroom. You could add some coloring sheets with color words on them to the small-motor center. Introducing color words with a children's book is always fun. *Brown Bear, Brown Bear, What Do You See?* (Bill Martin) is a favorite of mine.

Fluency

The main reason for reading is to comprehend meaning. If a child must stop to figure out many words, reading in "fits and starts," he/she will most likely find it difficult to get to meaning. Children must be able to read quickly and accurately; in this way, they become able to understand what is read. Fluency is more "caught" than "taught" at this level, meaning that students will hear others reading fluently rather than reading fluently themselves.

© McGraw-Hill Children's Publishing   0-7682-2920-0 *Getting Ready to Teach Reading for the New Teacher*

MODELING FLUENT READING

▶ Whenever you read anything to the children, you are modeling fluent reading.

▶ Fluent reading practice comes with choral reading and echo reading. In choral reading, you all chant something aloud together. In echo reading, the teacher reads something first and then the students repeat it.

▶ Using big books that have been developed for guided and shared reading are also a way to model fluency. (See page 52 for more on big books.)

▶ Have children who are able to read aloud do so often in the appropriate level emergent reader.

Tip There are several ways to expose children to fluency even if you are the only teacher in the classroom.

▶ Students can read with adult volunteers; the adults will be modeling fluency.

▶ Many schools match younger students with a student in an upper grade. Have the "buddy" read to kindergartner.

▶ Tape recordings at a listening center or individual tape players give children a chance to hear fluent reading.

▶ Reader's theater activities are another way to practice fluency through repeated practice saying their lines.

Questions for Comprehension

- What do you think will happen next?

- Why do you think this happened?

- What did you like about the story?

- Who were some of the characters in this story?

Comprehension

Can the children understand or draw meaning from the things they read or the things that are read to them? A kindergarten teacher starts the comprehension process by having many discussions about posters and pictures, big books, storybooks, and so on. With skillful questioning, the teacher draws attention to meaning.

Teaching of actual strategies for children to use while reading silently and independently is a skill better left to first grade. (Most of your competent early readers at the kindergarten level will already comprehend well anyway!)

COMPREHENSION ACTIVITIES

- A child could act out a scene from a story.
- Children could retell the story with a partner, to an adult, into a tape recorder, or by using puppets.
- Children could respond to a question or comment about a story through art. "Draw a picture of what happened to the Ugly Duckling in the winter."
- Children could complete a sentence about the story with their own spelling and then illustrate it. Putting these together makes a good class book. A sample sentence is: "The scariest thing that happened in the story was _____."

Concepts of Print and Book Sense

In addition to phonemic awareness, phonics, vocabulary, fluency, and comprehension, there are more general skills related to knowing and understanding what books are and how to use them. Some sample skills for kindergartners follow.

BOOK KNOWLEDGE

- Identify (point to) front cover, title page.
- Know where to locate the name of author and illustrator.

BOOK READING PROCEDURE

- Follow text from left to right, making the return sweep.
- Know that the print tells the story.
- Understand that sentences are made up of separate words (function of white space).
- Recognize the difference between individual letters and words.

EXPOSURE TO "CONVENTIONS"

- Recognize end-of-the-sentence marks—period, question mark, exclamation point.
- Notice capitalization of the first word in a sentence.
- Notice capitalization of a name.
- Notice use of quotation marks in print for conversation.

© McGraw-Hill Children's Publishing   0-7682-2920-0 *Getting Ready to Teach Reading for the New Teacher*

Putting It All Together with Big Books

Big books are a wonderful tool for teaching and reviewing many reading skills. Using them is one of the best ways to be sure your students are being exposed to concepts of print. Some big books are simply large copies of children's storybooks. These are wonderful to read for fluency and can be used for comprehension activities—and just to enjoy!

The big books most useful in teaching reading skills, however, are the ones developed specifically for shared and guided reading. They have a limited vocabulary, large print, predictable and often patterned text, and good illustrations.

You can use big books to review, to teach, and to expose children to various skills. It is probably the best way to enhance the concept of print with your class. Tips on using big books are below.

INTRODUCING THE BOOK

Some suggestions for using big books follow, along with a detail of the skills covered by that activity.

- Almost always read a new book *to* the children first, without having them respond or echo. Use this time to point out title, author, illustrator, title page. (concepts of print and book knowledge)
- Always use a pointer to go from left to right, return sweep, top to bottom. (concepts of print and book knowledge)
- Use the cover illustrations and any illustrations on the title page to ask children to predict what might happen, where the story appears to be set, and who it might be about. (comprehension skills, making predictions)
- Read the book fluently and with expression. (fluency)
- You could take a "detour" to explain a new vocabulary word or ask them to predict what might happen next. However, you will most frequently do this during rereading. (vocabulary, comprehension, and fluency)

Materials to Use Along with Big Books

- easel
- highlighting tape
- various pointers
- cardboard for framing letters or words

REREADING THE BOOK

▶ On the first rereading, have the children read with you or, perhaps, echo you.

▶ During subsequent rereadings, you can find opportunities to point out things such as capitalization of first words or names, periods, question marks, exclamation points.

▶ Indicate space between words, show what a sentence is, frame individual words.

ACTIVITIES WITH THE BOOK

These activities are appropriate with the whole class or with a small group during center time. You could group children by what skill they need to work on, too.

▶ Use highlighting tape and let children take turns sticking it on individual words, letters, or even on the space between words.

▶ Cut simple frames of different sizes from cardboard—colored index cards work fine—and attach a craft stick for a holder. Have children frame different words or letters.

▶ Have the children do choral reading or cloze activities.

Tip   My favorite big book to use is *Mrs. Wishy Washy* (Joy Cowley, Wright Group). Not only is this book popular with children, it gives you plenty of opportunities to point out almost all of the skills just mentioned. Children can do choral reading by being assigned to be an animal or Mrs. Wishy Washy. Trust me—they *will* read with expression when it is their turn! This book also has larger print to show loud voices, as well as quotation marks, exclamation points, and periods. I probably omitted a few other things you can do with this one!!

0-7682-2920-0 *Getting Ready to Teach Reading for the New Teacher*

BIG BOOK INNOVATIONS

Write the words to the story on separate sheets of paper and have the children illustrate the story their own way (in groups or individually). Be sure to write a title page that includes the words: Based on a book by _____.

Make class books from your big books. Use the book as a model for one you write and illustrate with your children. For example, instead of using Mrs. Wishy Washy and farm animals, your class could create a book about Mr. Zookeeper and zoo animals. You could make this a class writing project or make into a class book with each child making a page.

"Oh, lovely mud," said the
hippo and he *rolled* in it.

Tip   Put big books on your wish list, along with several student-size copies of the same story. In my opinion, they are one of the best beginning reading tools in classrooms today!

54

Chapter 4

Reading Aloud to Children

Why read to children? Jim Trelease has written an extremely popular book, *The Read-Aloud Handbook*, in part to give reasons and ideas for reading aloud to children. This book is an excellent resource meant for parents, but also of great value to teachers. To paraphrase Jim Trelease in the 1985 edition of his book, you read to children for the same reasons you talk to them. Reading aloud can reassure, entertain and inform, explain, arouse curiosity, and inspire them. He makes a big point of reading *personally* rather than with technology. This is a time to be enjoyed—both by you and the children!

0-7682-2920-0 *Getting Ready to Teach Reading for the New Teacher*

Reading aloud in the classroom is a great way to reinforce many of the reading skills already listed in this book. Most especially, it helps with fluency and comprehension. Vocabulary growth is an obvious reason to read to the children. Reading aloud is a time children enjoy and this can inspire them to become lifelong readers! Therefore, during the reading time, do not try to teach the skills in a way that will detract from the books.

Reading in Different Genres

Since most kindergartners are *not* independent readers, read-aloud time is a good time to introduce different genres. Choose a variety of books. Of course, storybooks will be used most often. But try to include some of the genres listed in the sidebar. Go ahead and give the books the genre labels before you read them: "Today we are reading a realistic fiction story; that is a story someone made up but it *could* happen in real life."

Another meaningful activity is to compare different versions of stories. Read a version of *Goldilocks and the Three Bears*, for instance. Another time, read *Goldilocks and the Three Hares* (Heidi Petach) or *Somebody and the Three Blairs* (Marilyn Tolhurst). Or, you could find several versions of the same folk tale—like *The Frog Prince* or *Stone Soup*.

Author Study

Is there a certain children's author you enjoy? Do an author study with your class. There is biographical information on the Internet about many children's book authors. Some appropriate authors for kindergartners are listed in the sidebar. The "study" can be informal, simply comparing the books after you have read them. If you have time, you could get more elaborate. You could add math—making a favorite book graph. You could make a simple mini-book for the children to complete (see page 111).

Genres for Kindergarten

- fiction
- folk tales and fairy tales
- fantasy
- poetry
- biography
- information books (nonfiction)
- nursery rhymes

Authors for Author Study

- Eric Carle
- Tomie De Paola
- Robert Kraus
- Mercer Mayer
- Leo Leonni
- Marcus Pfister
- Dr. Seuss

Reading Chapter Books

It is worth it to try to find the time to read chapter books to children. I know when teaching half-day classes, it may not be possible. It is also not easy to find appropriate chapter books for young children. Many schools have classroom reading lists that assign certain books to certain grades; you will want to avoid those books for your chapter book selections. In my school, for instance, I'm asked not to use *Charlotte's Web* (E. B. White) since the children will read it in another grade.

There are two series that I have used most successfully with my students. (After I read them the first time, the librarian had to order more copies because so many of my students wanted to hear them again at home!)

MY FATHER'S DRAGON

An old series that appeals to the need for fantasy and heroes is by Ruth Stiles Gannet: *My Father's Dragon* is followed by *Elmer and the Dragon* and *The Dragons of Blueland*. These books are old—the first one was published in 1948—but good! In fact, I find many opportunities for the children to learn the meanings of new words simply from outdated language: for instance, *knapsack* instead of *backpack*. One class was so excited about these books that they made a big book for the library, complete with dragons of all different patterns—but all with gold wings! I highly recommend this series to you.

> **Tip** When I use chapter books in a half-day program, I sometimes read while the children eat their snack—a handy time-saving technique.

0-7682-2920-0 *Getting Ready to Teach Reading for the New Teacher*

RUSSELL AND ELISA

The other series is a newer one by Johanna Hurwitz. The most appropriate books by this author are about a little boy and his sister named Russell and Elisa Michaels. The first book is *Rip-Roaring Russell*. A few of the other titles are listed in the Resources section (see page 137). The children will respond well to these books, even though some were written twenty years ago. They can relate to Russell and Elisa's growing pains: temper tantrums, new glasses, broken arms, sibling squabbles, new babies, moving. My students can hardly wait for the next chapter. Another nice thing about these books is that there are only six or seven fairly short chapters in each, so reading a chapter will not take too much of your day!

Using chapter books can give the teacher more opportunities to model fluency, enhance students' comprehension and vocabulary knowledge, and, most importantly, show the attitude that reading is WONDERFUL!

The children's book market has simply exploded in the last few years. New books are published constantly, and many are of wonderful quality. Sometimes, however, I find I overlook "oldies, but goodies" because I have eagerly purchased new books! I can't begin to keep up with it all. Listed in the resources are books I have used listed by alphabet letter of emphasis. I tried to limit myself to five books per letter. You will also find a list of alphabet books. (See resources section beginning on page 137.)

Read them (aloud) and have fun!!!

0-7682-2920-0 *Getting Ready to Teach Reading for the New Teacher*

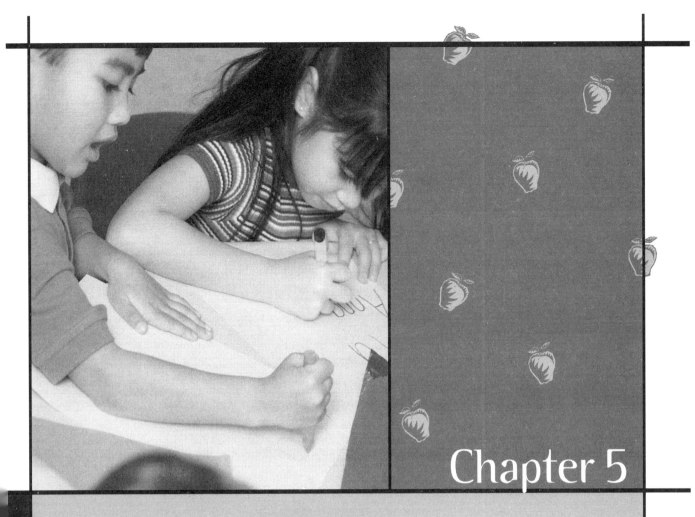

Chapter 5

Writing

Writing and reading go together in the classroom. At the kindergarten level, writing is a way for the children to put those phonics and other reading skills together and get their thoughts down on paper. Writing is probably the most brain-intensive activity the children will do in kindergarten. Since it is a grapho-motor skill, children with poor or immature motor skills may struggle, even though their readiness skills are fine!

Information on teaching writing could be a book in itself. The following section is a brief overview of the writing process in kindergarten, with a few suggested activities.

© McGraw-Hill Children's Publishing   0-7682-2920-0 *Getting Ready to Teach Reading for the New Teacher*

Forms of Writing in Kindergarten

PENMANSHIP (HANDWRITING)

As the children learn to recognize letters and sounds, it is natural to teach them how to form the letters correctly as well. Most teachers are given a prescribed handwriting curriculum they must use. The letters might have to be taught in a certain order according to the curriculum.

If you have any flexibility in the matter, I recommend that you teach the written letter when it is your "letter of emphasis" (see chapter 2). If you have already taught the letter in the formal handwriting curriculum, you could use the "letter of emphasis" time for review.

Letter formation charts should be available both on the wall and on the tables for students to see uppercase and lowercase letters. Get the children writing the lowercase letters as soon as possible. I say this for the following reasons:

▶ Many children come to school already writing most of the capital letters (perhaps not as your series recommends, but at least legibly).

▶ When we ask children to write sentences or words, we ask them to use lowercase, since that's what written English uses most frequently.

▶ The children will need the capitals, but not as often as the lowercase letters. If they write with all capitals in journals, for instance, it is difficult to break them of the habit later.

▶ Most schools require that children master the correct writing of their first names (with only the first letter capitalized) in kindergarten. Some schools require last name, too.

Remember that handwriting includes work on small-motor muscles in general. Writing letters can and should be done any way—with tracing paper, in sand or salt trays, with clay, in the air, on each other's backs, in shaving cream. Any sort of practice using these muscles is valuable—especially if it's fun, too!

0-7682-2920-0 *Getting Ready to Teach Reading for the New Teacher*

SHARED WRITING—*Teacher-Modeled Writing*

This is the first and probably the most important kind of writing for the children to see and experience. A morning message that is already written when students come in is *not* the idea. Teacher-modeled writing is when the teacher deliberately plans for and carries out a writing activity in front of the class. It can be written on a chalkboard, white board, or (preferably) on chart paper.

As you write, you are modeling many of the concepts of print. Get used to "talking your way through your writing."

"Today I am going to write about what a beautiful day it is.
<u>It</u> <u>is</u> <u>sunny</u> <u>and</u> <u>warm</u> <u>today</u>.
Let's see, I wrote six words."

Take the opportunity to teach/point out going left to right, top to bottom, return sweep. You do not have to do everything in every lesson, of course, but over the course of months, keep all of the concepts of print in mind.

Also, take the opportunity to write in different "genres." One day, you could write a list, another day a poem. Tell the children when you are writing information (nonfiction), fiction, or fantasy.

"Let's see. I wrote about a pig who is talking.
That's fantasy, when an animal talks."

Be sure to revise your writing on occasion.
"It is sunny and very warm today and that makes me happy."

Class-Dictated Stories—Experience Stories

These are the kinds of stories you write after field trips or special events (and other times, too, of course). Usually, writing the children's sentences on chart paper is a good start. You will do some rereading or echo reading of these stories. You might even follow up by having students make illustrations for the story to make a class book. Children also love to have photos in the books—especially photos of themselves on class trips!

0-7682-2920-0 *Getting Ready to Teach Reading for the New Teacher*

Sentences Dictated by Individuals

This is writing shared one-on-one. Especially early in the year, this is a good way to get children's ideas down on paper. First, children illustrate their idea. Then you write down what they want the paper to say!

Sentence Completion

Give each child a paper with a sentence started on it. They complete the sentence in their own spelling. Consider this: do we write the correct spelling on child-created books as well as the children's invented spelling? My answer: most of the time, when the book is going to be read by others. They will need to have exposure to some standard spelling. You can explain this to your class by saying that all authors need to revise and edit their writing! You will be modeling this when you write. You could even put a "revision" line on the student page. A sample page might look like this:

> In the fall, I like to _____ jmp in lvs
>
>
> In the fall, I like to _____ *jump in leaves.*
>
> (Revised by _Em_ and Miss Vander Woude.)

JOURNAL WRITING (DRAFT BOOK)

Individual children write in a notebook of some kind. The ideas are generated by the children themselves. Some children may have difficulty thinking of topics. You could send home a "Things I Can Write About" sheet for students to fill out with an adult helper (see page 107), or have an "Ideas to Write About" list that you create at school.

© McGraw-Hill Children's Publishing   0-7682-2920-0 *Getting Ready to Teach Reading for the New Teacher*

Journal writing should occur frequently; however, a realistic expectation for a new teacher of a half-day class is having the children write in their journals once a week. It is important to model the writing process before giving the children their own journals.

- Show the children that they should first get an idea and draw a small, simple sketch of that idea on their page. (**Plan**)
- Then, they do their writing. (**Do**)
- While waiting to read their writing to the teacher, they may go back and add details and color to the sketch. (**Review**)

These steps are taken from an article in the September/October 2002 edition of *Library Talk* titled "The Big6™: No Student Is Too Young." By emphasizing this procedure, you might be able to prevent your budding artists from spending the whole time drawing!

Developmental Stages of Spelling

You will see many emergent levels in your classroom. Each child's level is *fine* for that time! However, you should also see progress toward the next level(s) during the school year.

- Pictures only.
- Pictures and a few scrawls—scribble writing.
- Pictures and a few letters appear, often the letters of their name used over and over and in different order. You might even see a few numbers!
- Writing becomes random strings of letters.
- Writing shows some letter/sound match, usually initial consonant sounds.
- Words have more than one sound represented.
- Writers begin to add spaces.
- Spaces, some punctuation, longer sentences, and some correctly spelled words appear!

By the end of the year, you will probably have children spanning these levels.

Draft Books

This kind of writing is like journal writing, but also involves a revision, editing, and publishing step. The procedure could be as follows.

- Children think of an idea, draw their plan (sketch), and write their "story."
- The draft book is then placed in a bin and the teacher calls each child individually.
- The child "reads" the story to the teacher.
- The teacher writes the words in a simple booklet and the child rereads, using the edited version.
- The booklet is illustrated and becomes one of the child's published books.

This procedure might be quite difficult for a new teacher with no classroom aide. While the publishing goes on, the children work on other activities, or perhaps in centers. It is important to get to the publishing step as soon as possible. Many children will forget what they have written if you wait until the next day. As they become more secure in using letters/sounds, it becomes much easier to "translate" the writing.

Writing as a Form of Reading Assessment

Writing can tell a teacher much about a child's reading skills. If you see that a child has a good knowledge of letters and sounds in writing work, this is a good indication that the child can *read* those letters and sounds. Sometimes, assessing the "concepts of print" development of a child can be done almost exclusively through looking at writing. Occasionally, however, a child who truly has mastered letters and sounds has poor grapho-motor skills and can't remember how to form the letters. This indicates other concerns—but look at what you've learned about that child just through the writing!

Materials in Individual Writing Folders

- draft book
- letter chart
- published books
- "Things to Write About" sheet (see page 107)

© McGraw-Hill Children's Publishing

0-7682-2920-0 *Getting Ready to Teach Reading for the New Teacher*

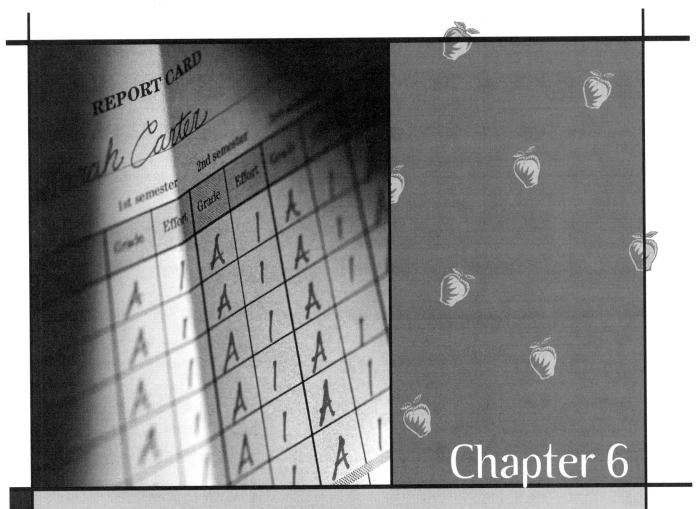

Chapter 6

Assessment

Every kindergarten teacher must find out what skills a child already has and what skills the child still needs to further develop literacy understanding. Knowing how to assess each child in a timely fashion is not always easy. For any teacher, especially a beginning teacher, this task can be daunting. This chapter will offer practical tips including organizing student records, finding time for assessment, and using assessment tools that are valuable, but not intimidating for the student (or the teacher!).

0-7682-2920-0 *Getting Ready to Teach Reading for the New Teacher*

Organization Essentials

SET UP FOLDERS (PORTFOLIOS)

One way to do this is to use a simple file folder with the child's name on it. You can place all of your assessment sheets in this folder. A hanging file to store the file folders in is also helpful. You can store samples of the child's work in the hanging file without having everything mixed in the folder with the assessment sheets.

Some schools provide teachers with portfolios for each child, and even have requirements of what you must include. You can add sheets for math assessment to these folders, too.

> **Tip** Consider filing the folders alphabetized by *first* name. Aides or volunteers who help you file work samples will most likely know the children by first name only.

MAKE COPIES OF THE RECORD-KEEPING SHEETS

Fill out names, addresses, and other required information ahead of time. See sample assessment forms on pages 71–80. You could make copies of all of the sheets you will use during the year and staple them into a booklet. If that is too time-consuming at the beginning of the year, simply copy one category at a time. However, be sure to write the child's name on each sheet individually. If you are anything like me, you'll occasionally misfile something when you're distracted.

INCLUDE A BLANK SHEET OF PAPER

Taping a blank sheet to the inside of the file folder is a great way to record informal observations. You could even just write on the inside of the folder itself, but I prefer to have my anecdotal comments on a paper that can be moved elsewhere if necessary.

That's about all you'll need to get started. Now, for a plan on how do to the assessments.

0-7682-2920-0 *Getting Ready to Teach Reading for the New Teacher*

Who Should Do the Assessing?

The classroom teacher should do all or most of the assessment for the following reasons:

▶ You can keep the assessments consistent.

▶ You will not need to talk to the outside assessor; you'll see and hear it all firsthand.

▶ You are the trained professional.

▶ You know the children best, and they will be most comfortable with you.

▶ Confidentiality: parent volunteers should not be put in a position where they can judge a child and perhaps inadvertently talk to another parent about that child's ability level.

Exception: if you are lucky enough to have a hired classroom aide, the aide could do some of the assessments for you!

Different Kinds of Assessment to Include

INFORMAL OBSERVATIONS

This is the first and most important assessment; it will be done continually. Do not, however, set yourself up for frustration by trying to do too much too soon. Watch the children, especially as they work/play in the centers. Listen to their language and see how they relate to others. Try to jot down at least one observation about each child by the end of the first full week.

Some teachers like to carry a clipboard or have it nearby for easy access. They make a grid to jot notes in, with a box for each child. Later, they transfer the notes to the assessment folder. Others like to use sticky notes to stick on the clipboard.

Remember to spend time enjoying the children and even joining in the activities. You should not have to use every spare minute for assessments. Kindergarten is more than getting ready for first grade. It is life itself, meant to be enjoyed and explored by everyone in the classroom, even the teacher!

© McGraw-Hill Children's Publishing

ASSESSING WITH WORKSHEETS

Occasionally, it is time-saving to give a special worksheet to each child and keep it to assess later or share with parents. A sample is included (see pages 71–73). How do you know if a child is copying from another? After all, we encourage kindergartners to help each other most of the time! When I do this sheet with my students we play a "secret mission" game. It's a bit corny, but it works. I separate the children as much as possible. The "game": do all the writing without letting ANYONE see!

WRITING FOLDER AND WORK SAMPLES

Use the writing folder and other work samples to assess a child's progress. The "Box Four" technique and the writing folder are described earlier (see pages 46 and 64). Be sure to add dates whenever possible to student work to help you track progress over time. This is easy to forget but very important!

INDIVIDUAL ASSESSMENT

The teacher works with each child individually, recording the responses. This can be a time where you present a specific written inventory, a series of oral directions, or another assessment tool. Sample assessments can be found on pages 71–80.

Finding Time for Assessment

Know that you are not going to get a lot of individual assessment done in the first month of school. If you have an aide, a bit is possible, but you will be busy establishing routines, introducing materials, setting rules, and reassuring children. You will find things out about most of the children informally. You'll soon pick out a child who reads a few words, as well as a child who talks all the time and has a wonderful vocabulary. For some children, you could fill out a page a day, but for most, you will get to know them gradually and as you pull them aside for assessment. They usually enjoy the time alone with you, especially if you keep the sessions short and nonthreatening.

Some children get a bit nervous during assessment, especially when they feel inadequate or frustrated. So, before I assess, I tell them that the reason we are going to talk together is to find out what I, the teacher, need to do to teach better! That puts the burden on me and often a reluctant child will be less anxious and risk more answers.

At the kindergarten level, a couple of ways to assess usually work well. After your learning centers (the kind considered "free play") are operating well, use the time to work individually with one or two children each session. If you decide to use literacy or reading centers as described in this book, you could use the time (perhaps for a whole week) to assess while the children work. Interruptions will probably occur, but that's life in kindergarten!

Try to assess the children in alphabet letter recognition and rhyming first (see pages 74 and 75). These screenings go very quickly, since many children recognize all of the letters right away. When you have a child who misses all or most of the first ten, you might as well stop for that day and try again a few weeks later.

I prefer to screen the whole class on alphabet recognition, and then go through the class again on rhyming skills. That way, you only work with each child for a few minutes; they'll want to get back to their work or play!

Once you have screened for these two skills, you'll already have quite a bit of information. You will not only have lists of children needing work in some skills, you will be able to use big books and other tools more appropriately. Note: Children who do not do well on rhyming often have difficulty with other PA or phonics skills. While this can be developmental, be sure to observe this child closely over the next few months.

Why Are We Doing All This Assessing?

In a nutshell, here's why:

▶ to get to know the students
▶ to plan for curriculum to include differentiating instruction at times
▶ to stay accountable
▶ to report to parents
▶ to gather data for child's cumulative file

© McGraw-Hill Children's Publishing   0-7682-2920-0 *Getting Ready to Teach Reading for the New Teacher*

To Rubric or Not to Rubric?

The assessment pages to follow are not based on rubrics. Rubrics are most effective when they are teacher-designed, or provided by a particular reading series or program. If you are required to use rubrics for your assessing, there is a lot of information on the Internet. Use a search engine such as google.com and type in the words "Kindergarten Rubrics." You will get examples of rubrics, information about rubrics, and more.

The following pages have assessment sheets you could use with your students. Notice that there are sheets for you to keep records on and a few sheets for the children to use during the assessment sessions. The assumption is that the children will make progress on their skills during the year. The ultimate would be if every child was correct on all of the responses by the end of the year. That won't happen except in the ideal world. As a matter of fact, it is normal to have children at many different developmental levels. *We must resist making the assumption that all children must learn to read at the same time!* Use the assessment sheets to follow a child's progress. Later in the school year, you might find a child who is having difficulty in several areas or showing no progress in one skill. Interventions for such scenarios are in the next chapter.

"The goal . . . is not to encourage parents and preschool teachers to teach children to read and write conventionally before first grade. Some children who have the kinds of experiences described in this book learn to read during preschool or the kindergarten years. Others do not begin to read and write until they are in first grade. But all children benefit from experiences that help build the necessary foundation for learning to read and write."

—*Much More Than the ABC's, Judith A. Schickedanz, page 9 (emphasis mine)*

SECRET MISSION ASSESSMENT SHEET TEACHER GUIDE

The directions below refer to the student pages that follow.

STUDENT PAGE 1

1. Write your name on the line by the pencil. Shhh, keep it a secret!

2. I'll say each picture out loud. Then you write down some letters you hear on the line under the picture. Listen carefully. Shhh, keep it a secret! (One by one, say the following words: *cat, frog, pizza, elephant.*)

STUDENT PAGE 2

1. I'm going to ask you to draw some shapes on the line at the top of the page. Try to keep them small, because this is a secret mission. Here are the shapes to draw: circle, square, triangle, diamond, rectangle.

2. Your last secret assignment is to draw a picture. The picture must be of a person next to a tree.

ASSESSING THE RESULTS

What you can learn about the children from these two pages:

▶ How well can they follow directions?

▶ Can they write their first names? Do they write their first name with capital on first letter only?

▶ Emergent writing level: Is there some letter/sound correspondence? Can the child write down at least the beginning sound? Do they still use scribbles?

▶ Handwriting: Are there lots of reversals? (Not a concern yet, just make note of it.) Does the child make wobbly letters? Does the child write few, if any, letters?

▶ Small-motor control: The shapes section will give you an idea about math vocabulary and also a feel for their small-motor maturity. Triangles and diamonds are tough for some children!

▶ The picture: Look for maturity in the drawings. (Some children just don't like to draw, so this task might not tell you too much about those kinds of kids.)

McGraw-Hill Children's Publishing   0-7682-2920-0 *Getting Ready to Teach Reading for the New Teacher*

Secret Mission—Student Page 1

Directions: Write your name here. Be sure to use your best writing.

_____

Directions: Write the letters you hear in each word, using your own spelling.

_____

_____

_____

_____

© McGraw-Hill Children's Publishing
0-7682-2920-0 *Getting Ready to Teach Reading for the New Teacher*

Secret Mission—Student Page 2

Directions: Draw the shapes. Listen carefully!

Draw a person next to a tree.

© McGraw-Hill Children's Publishing   0-7682-2920-0 *Getting Ready to Teach Reading for the New Teacher*

ASSESSMENT RECORDING SHEET

Child's Name _____ Date _____

Identifying Information
Mark box if child can recite it. Write response on the line.

☐ Name _____

☐ Address _____

☐ Telephone Number _____

☐ Birth Date _____

Letter Recognition
Give child the sheet of letters (see page 77). Ask child to point to each letter and give its name. On the recording form below, circle the letters the child gets correct. Discontinue if the child misses more than six in a row. Try again at a later time. Date each attempt. You could use a different color ink each time you assess the child—that way it's easy to spot the progress and you can reuse the form.

Date _____ Date _____ Date _____ Date _____

O	S	A	H	E	W	I	P	L
B	Q	U	Z	C	T	G	X	N
R	J	Y	M	F	D	K	V	

Date _____ Date _____ Date _____ Date _____

a	o	s	h	e	i	d	f	m
q	t	r	b	u	c	g	w	l
y	p	k	n	z	j	x	v	

0-7682-2920-0 *Getting Ready to Teach Reading for the New Teache*

ASSESSMENT RECORDING SHEET

Child's Name _____ Date _____

The rhyming assessment has two parts: rhyme recognition and rhyme supply. While most children do best at first with rhyme recognition, sometimes a child actually does better on rhyme supply. Therefore, screen for both skills.

Rhyme Recognition

Use the script below to give examples first. Then go through the list of words, putting a check in front of the pair of words if the child is correct. If child misses three in a row, stop and try again another time.

"Some words sound nearly the same: *man* and *fan*. *Man* and *fan* rhyme because they end the same way. Listen again: *man*, *fan*. Now listen to some more words. Tell me 'yes' if they rhyme, 'no' if they don't."

miss	kiss	peep	creep
sock	sit	ball	fall
rat	sat	book	head

Rhyme Supply

Accept non-words, as long as they rhyme. For example: *pill*, *zill*. Stop if no response after four.

"First I say *pill* and then I say *hill*. *Pill* and *hill* rhyme. Now you tell me a word that rhymes."

Write down the child's response.	
cat _____	ship _____
run _____	rose _____
bed _____	box _____
try _____	sad _____

© McGraw-Hill Children's Publishing   0-7682-2920-0 *Getting Ready to Teach Reading for the New Teacher*

ASSESSMENT RECORDING SHEET

Child's Name _____ Date _____

Letter Sounds

Use the same sheet for students that was used in the letter recognition assessment (see page 77). Ask the child to point to each letter and give the *sound* of the letter. You may have to demonstrate. Use a letter from the last row. Circle correct responses. Stop after about half if the child is missing most. However, you could also skip the vowels the first time and use only consonants, which are a bit easier.

Date _____		Date _____		Date _____		Date _____		
a	o	s	h	e	i	d	f	m
q	t	r	b	u	c	g	w	l
y	p	k	n	z	j	x	v	

Beginning Sounds of Words 1—Sound Screening

Read each word to the child. Ask child to tell you the first *sound*. For example: What is the first sound of *cat*? The following ten words should be enough. You will know quite quickly if a child can separate the initial phoneme. Circle correct responses.

Date _____				
dad	fire	help	violin	tent
kite	mouth	wagon	sand	ant

Beginning Sounds of Words 2—Letter Screening (optional)

Read each word to the child. Child should give the letter *name* of the first letter. If child says "c" for *kite*, ask if child knows another letter it could be. Use the same procedure for "s/c" and "j/g." The vowels are more difficult for many children and could be skipped until later.

mouth	box	popcorn	cup	new
jump	zoo	yellow	quick	ant

0-7682-2920-0 *Getting Ready to Teach Reading for the New Teacher*

Name _____ Date _____

Letter Recognition and Letter Sounds

Directions: **Letter Recognition:** Point to each letter and give its name. You may say "pass" if you don't know, and that's okay!

Directions: **Letter Sounds:** Give me the sound of each letter. You may say "pass" if you don't know, and that's okay!

O	S	A	H	E	W
I	P	L	B	Q	U
Z	C	T	G	X	N
R	J	Y	M	F	D
K	V				

a	o	s	h	e	i
d	f	m	q	t	r
b	u	c	g	w	l
y	p	k	n	z	j
x	v				

© McGraw-Hill Children's Publishing   0-7682-2920-0 *Getting Ready to Teach Reading for the New Teacher*

ASSESSMENT RECORDING SHEET

Child's Name _____ Date _____

Sounds Assessment

Ask the child the following questions. Discontinue any of the screenings if child misses several in a row or appears frustrated or confused.

What sound does your name start with? _____

Can you think of another word that starts like that? _____

Do these words start with the same sound? Tell me "yes" or "no."

man   mouse _____   tan   party _____

bed   boy _____   shop   shin _____

Tell me a word that begins with this letter's sound. (Make simple index cards with each letter on one card to show to the child one at a time.)

t _____   f _____   l _____

m _____   s _____   p _____

Blending

Pronounce the words separately as divided. Ask the child to blend the sounds together to make a word. (This screening should be done only after the children have lots of practice doing it in school with you. See the blender activity on page 40.) There is no "minimum" number for a child to get right, but this screening will tell you which children might be ready to sound out simple words.

Tell the child:

"I am going to say two sounds: /a/ and /m/. I blend them together and say 'am.' Now, you try it with these words." (The words below have a bullet to separate the sounds as you should say them.)

Date _____

| i · l | m · an | sh · o · p | i · f | r · un | tr · ick |
| u · p | c · ot | fl · a · p | s · o | d · id | dr · i · p |

0-7682-2920-0 *Getting Ready to Teach Reading for the New Teacher*

ASSESSMENT RECORDING SHEET

Child's Name _____ Date _____

Discontinue any of the screenings if child misses several in a row or appears frustrated or confused.

Segmenting

The following screening is probably not for all students, since segmentation is a skill more appropriate for first grade. However, you might have some students who could do this in kindergarten.

The child is asked to take the words apart. Give an example: "If I take the word *dog* apart, I would hear this: /d/ /o/ /g/. Now you try to take apart these words." Write child's response on line, indicating letter sound divisions.

ham _____   mop _____

dip _____   red _____

soup _____   that _____

soon _____   stop _____

Onset and Rime

Ask the child: "What word would I have if I put these sounds together?" Write the child's response on the line.

c · ake _____   m · ad _____

t · in _____   j · ump _____

l · og _____   t · ent _____

b · at _____   sh · ut _____

c · up _____   b · ike _____

McGraw-Hill Children's Publishing   0-7682-2920-0 *Getting Ready to Teach Reading for the New Teacher*

Child's Name _____

ASSESSMENT	RESULT (DATE)	COMMENTS
Identifying Information *name* *address* *telephone* *birth date*		
Letter Recognition *capital* *lowercase*		
Rhyming *recognition* *supply*		
Letter Sounds		
Beginning Letters		
Blending		
Segmenting		
Onset and Rime		
Concepts of Print		
Does well in:		
Should work on:		

0-7682-2920-0 *Getting Ready to Teach Reading for the New Teach*

Chapter 7

Meeting Special Needs

Every child in your class deserves to be challenged at his or her own level—of development, interest, and skill. It is comforting to know that so many of the techniques kindergarten teachers routinely use meet the varied needs of so many children. For instance, using learning centers means children are able to choose what to do and work at their own pace. You do not have to do much more for most students than provide a stimulating, activity-filled environment, with times of choice, times of whole-group community-building activities, and times of small-group work. For those students who truly need special intervention, however, this chapter will give you practical tips for providing them with what they need.

0-7682-2920-0 *Getting Ready to Teach Reading for the New Teacher*

A multisensory and integrated curriculum meets the needs of children with different learning styles. And since kindergarten is more than academics, many of the activities meet social and emotional needs as well. There are other ways to provide for individual needs. As you do assessment, you will find children who need to work on similar skills. These children can be grouped together to work on the skill as a group with you—using a pocket chart, book, or game, for instance.

But what about the children who have special needs?

Intervention for At-Risk Students

These are the students that worry you; after assessing them, you find they have many areas that seem to show slow development of skills.

INVOLVE THE PARENTS IMMEDIATELY

This can be one of the most difficult conversations to have with parents. Always try to start by mentioning the ways the child *is* succeeding and how much you care about their child. Gently bring up specific concerns that indicate to you that some further assessment by school specialists might be helpful so that you can plan the very best curriculum for their child. Each school's referral system probably varies a bit. Most schools follow steps like these.

- Meet with the parents. Show work samples and discuss your assessment results. Get parent permission to seek input from colleagues, especially resource room personnel.
- Discuss child with colleague, followed by classroom observations by that colleague.
- Further assessment by specialists if indicated.
- Meet with parents to discuss results.
- Make an individual curriculum plan for the child and implement it.

0-7682-2920-0 *Getting Ready to Teach Reading for the New Teache*

"We must intervene early to help ensure that a child will become a fluent reader. What nature hasn't built, schools can help to build."
—Sally Shaywitz, *"On the Mind of a Child," Educational Leadership,* April 2003

The key to intervening for special needs is having open communication with *all* parents from day one. Classroom newsletters are great for this. Special notes or calls home can be helpful as you begin to have concerns. By the time a true problem arises, parents should trust you and feel like a partner in their child's education. This can be a very painful time for parents! But early intervention is much better than having to remediate at a later grade.

Intervention for Students with Just a Few Difficulties

What about those children having difficulty in just one or two areas? It is very easy to become alarmed too soon at the kindergarten level. Very often, a "lag" in some skill is developmental for that child and not a cause of concern.

Many parents will ask what they can do at home to help their child. You might mention the fact that many educational publishers have series of workbooks that parents can use for review at home. McGraw-Hill's *Learn at Home* series is one you could suggest. There are some "Prescriptions for Parents" cards at the end of this chapter (see pages 86–89). These could be used in your newsletters, or they could be sent home to the parents of children who need work on a certain skill.

Another wonderful at-home activity is one that may have to wait until you have more materials. Get small copies of your class big books and let the children check them out to read at home. You could store them in bags with a note of explanation for the parents. (See sample letter on page 90).

© McGraw-Hill Children's Publishing 0-7682-2920-0 *Getting Ready to Teach Reading for the New Teacher*

Enrichment Activities for High-Achieving Students

You will likely have a child in kindergarten who reads and writes quite fluently. Once again, remember that the socialization activities you have built in to the kindergarten curriculum are important for this child, too. There are times you might like to broaden this child's experience. There are some simple things you could do without overextending yourself.

▶ Add more advanced writing activities to your writing center. Blank books work well for children at every level. Your more able students will be able to write short sentences rather than words.

▶ Put more advanced activities in your games center. Example: Add cards with words-only written on them for the child to match.

▶ Do buddy projects. Pair two very able students for a project. At other times, pair a more advanced student with a less advanced one.

▶ Rather than getting books just once a week during library time, allow a reader to check out new books as soon as the old ones are brought back to school.

▶ Introduce your class to doing research. Children with more advanced skills could actually write their own report. See the section below for more details.

Research in Kindergarten?

An article about research titled "The Big6™ or Super3—No Student Is Too Young" appeared in the September/October 2002 edition of *Library Talk* magazine. Information on the Big6 can be found at: www.big6.com.

Kindergartners can be taught to use the Super3 (from the above source).

Plan: What do we want to find out?
Do: Do the research with books or pictures.
Review: What did we find out and how will we tell others?

0-7682-2920-0 *Getting Ready to Teach Reading for the New Teache*

Suppose your class wants to find out about worms. Find a simple book, such as *The Earthworm* (Wonder World set, Wright Group). Many good emergent books are available from various sources nowadays. What do we want to find out about worms? (**Plan**) Help the children make a web or chart, such as the one below. Notice that the chart has both words and pictures so children of all abilities can paricipate in this activity. They (and you) suggest categories.

Read the book to the children. (**Do**) Fill in the chart as part of the discussion afterwards. Then, have them help you write a report by putting the answers to your questions in sentence form. This report could be typed up and duplicated. Each child could have a copy and illustrate it. (**Review**) This process does not always have to result in a chart or a report. Simply going through information books occasionally is good practice for the children.

Where live?	Bodies
Babies	What need to live
What are they good for?	Questions?

I put the topic of research in this section rather than in comprehension, because it is not basic to the kindergarten curriculum, but would be a wonderful thing for an advanced child to do individually, perhaps in a writing center. With an information book on the child's chosen topic and a small copy of the chart above, such a child could write his or her own notes in the boxes—yes, note-taking in kindergarten! A report could be made verbally to the class, or the teacher could make arrangements for the child to dictate the report to an adult. It would take some extra work on your part, but what a wonderful experience for a gifted child.

0-7682-2920-0 *Getting Ready to Teach Reading for the New Teacher*

Prescriptions for Parents

Help Your Child at Home

These cards could be sent home with children for use at home, given to parents when they ask how they can help their child, and/or put in parent newsletters.

COMPREHENSION AND VOCABULARY

▶ Read to your child daily.

▶ Discuss the story or ask a few questions.

▶ Talk about the meaning of at least one word.

▶ Try having a "word of the week" with your family. For example: "There are *blossoms* on the tree. *Blossom* can mean a flower, or it can mean to grow blossoms."

WORD PLAY—GETTING TUNED INTO SOUNDS!

This skill will help when your child needs to learn to "sound out words."

Ask your child to think of as many animals as he or she can. Then, say just the first sound of the animal and see if you can guess it. Take turns doing this! For example: "I'm thinking of an animal that starts with /p/."

You could do this on another day with another category, such as foods.

SYLLABLES

Syllables are the "beats" of words. Teach your child the meaning of the word as well as the number of syllables. Have fun stamping, clapping, or tapping out the syllables!

Say the word *beautiful*. Clap out the syllables with your child. Now do more words that way. Take turns with your child. Any words will do! Can you think of some four- or five-syllable words?

It's really fun if you get something like jingle bells and ring out the syllables. Or, if you can stand it, let your child use a pan lid and a spoon to "gong" out the syllables.

YOU CAN NEVER HAVE TOO MUCH RHYME!

▶ Read rhyming books often; this helps your child learn to find patterns in the sounds of our language

▶ Play rhyming games. Let your child use "nonsense" rhymes (not real words).

▶ Try it two ways: ask your child if two words you say rhyme or not. Do *man* and *fan* rhyme? Do *man* and *mat* rhyme? Then ask your child how many words he/she can think of that rhyme with _____.

0-7682-2920-0 *Getting Ready to Teach Reading for the New Teach*

Prescriptions for Parents
Help Your Child at Home

WORD PLAY: GETTING TUNED IN TO SOUND AGAIN!

The following practice will help when your child begins to sound out and spell words.

Tell your child: "Oops! These words got cut apart; can you put them back together again?" Read the following words, divided as indicated. (For c · ab, you'd say "cuh" "ab." Your child would say "cab.") Feel free to think of more words!

s · ob	b · ig	f · an	b · ib
f · ire	j · ump	r · ub	b · ed

COMPREHENSION

Read a book and ask questions about it. Choose a book you're familiar with, or else look at the book ahead of time.

Help your child plan ahead. Example: Choose a Berenstain Bear book, perhaps. Say to your child before you read: "When the story is over, I'm going to ask you to tell me three things that Papa Bear did that got him into trouble. Listen carefully."

Some books, if unfamiliar to your child, are wonderful for asking him/her to predict what is going to happen next.

DRAW AND WRITE

Have your child draw a picture, and then talk about it. Then, your child should write something about that picture in his or her own spelling. Don't worry if words are not spelled correctly! He or she should then read the sentence to you.

Acknowledge the wonderful effort. Then, work to edit the work. You rewrite the sentence in correct spelling. Label it: "Writing edited by Mom and (your child's name)."

VOCABULARY GROWTH (SYNONYMS)

This can be done orally or you may write down your child's responses. (You do not have to mention the term *synonyms*.)

Select a word: "Let's see how many words we can think of that mean just about the same thing as _____."

Suggestions:

nice   hot   fun   great   cold

0-7682-2920-0 *Getting Ready to Teach Reading for the New Teacher*

Prescriptions for Parents
Help Your Child at Home

ALPHABET LETTER NAMES

Write the alphabet in order on a sheet of paper or a card. Make one sheet of capitals and one of lowercase letters.

▶ Sing the alphabet song slowly (or just say the letters) and have your child point to each letter. Use a pencil, straw, or something else as a pointer.

▶ Now, have your child say the alphabet alone.

▶ Later, play "Name Me." Point to the letters in random order, having your child name the letters as quickly as he or she can.

ALPHABET LETTER SOUNDS

Point to the letters. Have your child make the *sound* of the letter (not give the *name* of the letter).

Optional: Circle the sounds the child knows. Make a different sheet with the sounds he or she still needs to work on. Have the child repeat the sound as you point to each letter.

SEARCH THE HOUSE!

▶ In this game, you wander through the rooms of your house, naming objects and giving the beginning sound of the object.

▶ Second option: Child gives the letter name of the object.

▶ Third option: Find things starting with a certain sound. For example, find objects starting with the same sound as your child's name.

I CAN READ!

Use a spiral notebook or staple some papers together to make a booklet.

Using magazines, newspaper ads, or even things like napkins or cereal and cracker boxes, have your child cut out words or logos he/she can read and glue them on the pages. This is a book your child will like to add to and "read" often.

Another use for this book is to have your child circle or point to the beginning letter of each word.

0-7682-2920-0 *Getting Ready to Teach Reading for the New Teacher*

Prescriptions for Parents
Help Your Child at Home

STICKER FUN

Get a set or two of stickers that have a variety of pictures. Use index cards.

Have your child pick a sticker and put it on a card. Write the word on a different card. Make a set of about ten cards. (Or, if you make more, only use ten cards at a time.)

Activities:

▶ Match the word with the picture.

▶ Sort the pictures by category (color, beginning sound, etc.).

▶ Use as a memory (concentration) game.

CONCEPTS OF PRINT

Here are things to find/do when you read. Don't do all of these at once!!

▶ Locate title, title page, author.

▶ Have your child follow the print going left to right. You may have to help.

▶ Find capital letters at beginning of sentences.

▶ Locate periods, quotation marks, question marks, and exclamation points.

▶ Find individual letters in words and identify them.

▶ Point to the first word on a page.

▶ Point to the spaces between words.

CUT UPS!

Make the following words on cards.

cat	hat	rat
bed	red	led
pig	wig	dig
hop	pop	top

If your child can read these words, GREAT! If not, you can still use this activity. Have your child cut off the first letter with a scissor. Then, slide the "word" back together and read it. Do this over and over. You might like to keep each set of rhyming words in separate envelopes to read again.

CAPITAL AND LOWERCASE MATCH

Use 26 index cards, cut in half to make 52.

Write the capital letter on one card and the lowercase letter on another.

Have your child match the capitals with the lowercase letters.

You might have to work with half of the letters at a time.

© McGraw-Hill Children's Publishing

0-7682-2920-0 *Getting Ready to Teach Reading for the New Teacher*

We have a classroom library with many beginning reading books called "emergent readers." These simple books have repetitive text and pictures to help a child figure out the words.

We have also used many big books in our class this year. The children will soon be given the opportunity to bring home a small copy of one of our big books. We'll use the above-mentioned books for a couple of weeks first.

Each child may bring home two books at a time. Books may be kept one week but can be returned sooner than that. A child may check out a book anytime; there are not certain days for this. Some children might not want to bring books home at this time.

Suggestions for Using the Books with Your Child

1. Have your child "read" the book to you. He or she might have memorized the book or might even just be telling you the gist of the story. That's fine! Still others might be able to read every word. *All of these levels are appropriate for a kindergarten class!*

2. Shared reading—read the book with your child. Read it slowly, but with expression, using your finger to go from left to right in each line.

3. The two above are important, but *enjoyment of the reading process is the goal*. However, if your child shows interest, you might do some of the following:

   ▶ Have your child count words in a sentence.

   ▶ Encourage your child to copy a sentence and make his/her own illustrations.

   ▶ Create a word scavenger hunt. Tell your child to find certain words, such as: *the, and, want, to, go.*

Thank you for your participation and happy reading!

Chapter 8

Last Words

To say that a first-year teacher is going to be busy is an understatement. I hope this book has given you some tips to make your life easier. You will be teaching many subjects besides reading. To repeat (again): try to teach thematically and by integrating the subjects. Save the "heavy" professional reading for next summer.

Work hard, but not so hard that you can't enjoy these wonderful children. Nothing can top the enthusiasm of a kindergartner (in my opinion!). Feed off their energy; share their joy of life. It's a two-way process, for you'll be sharing yourself with them, too. Have fun on your new adventure.

Kindergartners Can Read!

In closing, I am giving one last reading idea for you to use on one of the first days of school. You see, kindergartners already can read. Reading is much more than words. They can read:

◗ signs	◗ shapes
◗ faces	◗ times of the year
◗ numbers	◗ pictures
◗ letters	◗ colors
◗ names	◗ a few words

It's exciting for students to realize they already know how to read. Using the "I Can Read" big book and having students make their own small copies is a great way to instill reading confidence from the start of the year on!

"I Can Read" Big Book

Everything you need to make an "I Can Read" big book follows (see pages 94–104). There are also pages to make a student mini-book (see pages 105–106), which the children will be proud to read at home. You could enlarge this on a photocopier to make it bigger. Mount each page on 12" x 18" construction paper. Laminate when you have finished coloring it.

- **Cover**   Decorate cover with stickers of children if possible.
- **Page 2**   Color. Add logos such as McDonald's, local grocery stores, familiar snack items (use newspaper ads or napkins to find logos).
- **Page 5**   When reading this with the children, read it first in a-b-c order, then point to each one in random order.
- **Page 6**   Color each balloon a different color.
- **Page 9**   Use provided picture or find an interesting magazine picture.

0-7682-2920-0 *Getting Ready to Teach Reading for the New Teacher*

▶ **Page 10**—Add any other words your class might know. Keep it simple, so everyone can read it!

▶ **Page 11**—Write your class's first names. If you have two classes, write one on the back of the book, so that you do not have to make two books.

However, if you do make two books, it is great to send one home with the children on a rotating basis.

Already reading—and ready for more! That's kindergarten reading instruction!!

0-7682-2920-0 *Getting Ready to Teach Reading for the New Teacher*

I Can Read!
Our Kindergarten Reader

Signs

0-7682-2920-0 *Getting Ready to Teach Reading for the New Teacher*

Faces

0-7682-2920-0 *Getting Ready to Teach Reading for the New Teacher*

Numbers

7

100

4

3

2

9

6

5

1

8

10

4

0-7682-2920-0 *Getting Ready to Teach Reading for the New Teacher*

Letters

Aa	Bb	Cc
Dd	Ee	Ff
Gg	Hh	Ii
Jj	Kk	Ll
Mm	Nn	Oo
Pp	Qq	Rr
Ss	Tt	Uu
Vv	Ww	Xx
Yy	Zz	

© McGraw-Hill Children's Publishing
0-7682-2920-0 *Getting Ready to Teach Reading for the New Teache*

Colors

0-7682-2920-0 *Getting Ready to Teach Reading for the New Teacher*

Shapes

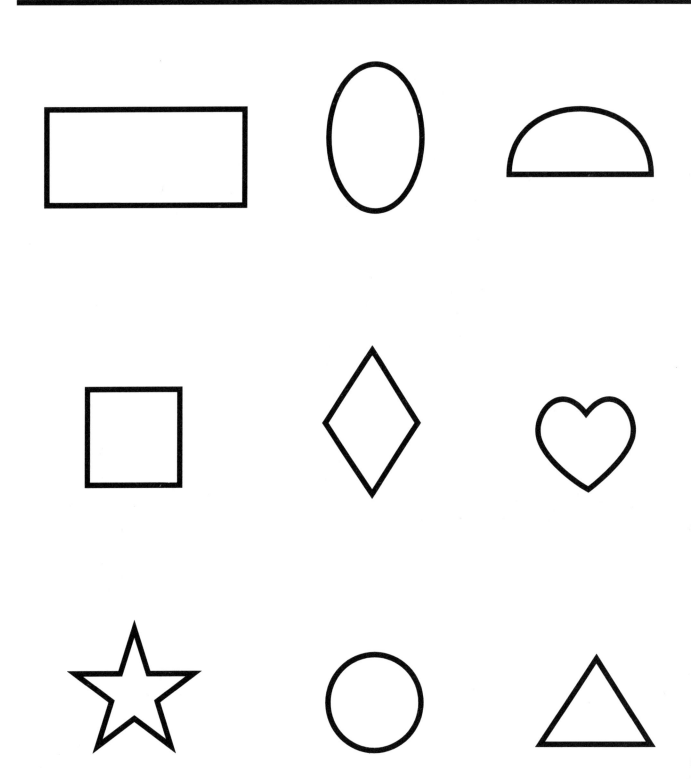

© McGraw-Hill Children's Publishing   0-7682-2920-0 *Getting Ready to Teach Reading for the New Teache*

Time of Year

McGraw-Hill Children's Publishing   0-7682-2920-0 *Getting Ready to Teach Reading for the New Teacher*

Pictures

9

0-7682-2920-0 *Getting Ready to Teach Reading for the New Teache*

Words

yes   no

dad   mom

dog   cat

McGraw-Hill Children's Publishing   0-7682-2920-0 *Getting Ready to Teach Reading for the New Teacher*

Names

0-7682-2920-0 *Getting Ready to Teach Reading for the New Teach*

I Can Read!

Our Kindergarten Reader

Names

Colors

Shapes

Letters

Aa	Bb	Cc	Dd	Ee
Ff	Gg	Hh	Ii	Jj
Kk	Ll	Mm	Nn	Oo
Pp	Qq	Rr	Ss	Tt
Uu	Vv	Ww	Xx	Yy
Zz				

© McGraw-Hill Children's Publishing

Numbers

10 6 5
3 2
4 1
8
100 7

Faces

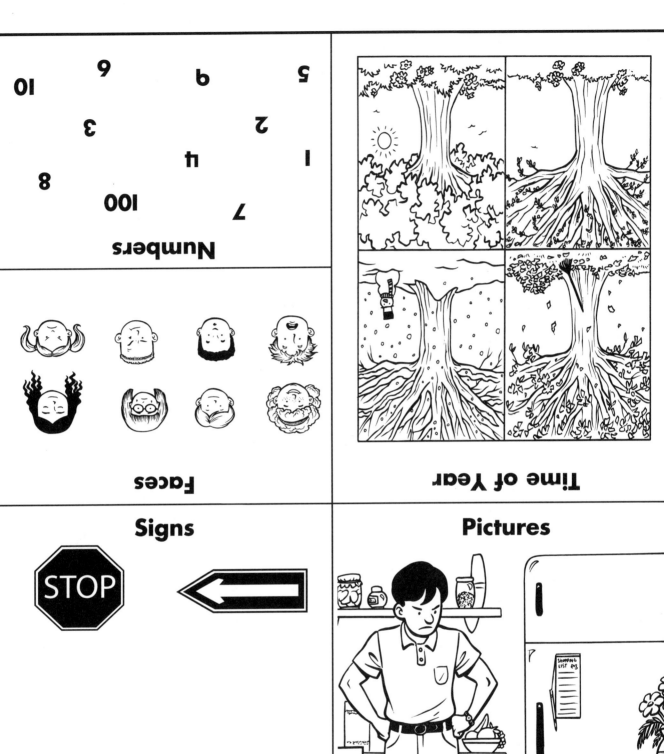

Time of Year

Signs

STOP

Pictures

Name _____ Date _____

Things I Can Write About

Directions: Ask a grown-up to help you think of things you might like to write about during the year. You might even include a few words to use for each topic. Use the questions to help you get started.

▸ Whose house do you like to visit?
▸ Do you have any pets (real or imaginary)?
▸ What is your favorite toy?

What to Write About	Words to Use

McGraw-Hill Children's Publishing   0-7682-2920-0 *Getting Ready to Teach Reading for the New Teacher*

Fall Fun

In the fall, I like to _____

In the fall, I like to _____

(Revised by teacher and student.)

School Things

by_____

Winter Wonders

by_____

I See Red!

by_____

I Like Blue

by_____

This author wrote lots of books. Here are some of them.

Here is something we learned about this author.

My favorite book by this author is _____.

My Author Book about

_____

Ask me what happened in the story. I'll explain my picture to you.

Amazing Maze

Directions: Follow the path of the maze. Use a pencil or stickers. Stay in the path!

0-7682-2920-0 *Getting Ready to Teach Reading for the New Teach*

See-Through Picture

Directions: Make a see-through picture! Put a piece of black paper under this one. Clip the papers together. Poke holes through the dots with a tack. When you are finished, hold the black paper up to the light. What do you see?

McGraw-Hill Children's Publishing   0-7682-2920-0 *Getting Ready to Teach Reading for the New Teacher*

Riding High

Directions: Connect the dots from **A** to **Z**.

0-7682-2920-0 *Getting Ready to Teach Reading for the New Teach*

Fly Away

Directions: Connect the dots from **a** to **z**.

McGraw-Hill Children's Publishing   0-7682-2920-0 *Getting Ready to Teach Reading for the New Teacher*

Firehouse

Directions: Color the path to the firehouse. Follow the alphabet from **A** to **Z**.

	A	B	C	D	E
	E	V	R	J	F
O	N	M	L	K	M	G
P	W	C	A	J	I	H
Q	R	S	T	D	F	N
I	G	X	U	V	W	X
O	K	N	S	L	H	Y
					Z

0-7682-2920-0 *Getting Ready to Teach Reading for the New Teacher*

On the Farm

Directions: Color the path to the barn. Follow the alphabet from **a** to **z**.

	a	t	o	p	q
	b	e	n	v	r
e	d	c	z	m	f	s
f	r	w	s	l	c	t
g	h	i	j	k	d	u
b	f	s	n	d	w	v
x	m	p	h	y	x	k
t	d	b	c	z		

117

0-7682-2920-0 *Getting Ready to Teach Reading for the New Teacher*

Letter Leaves

Directions: Draw lines to match the uppercase and lowercase letters.

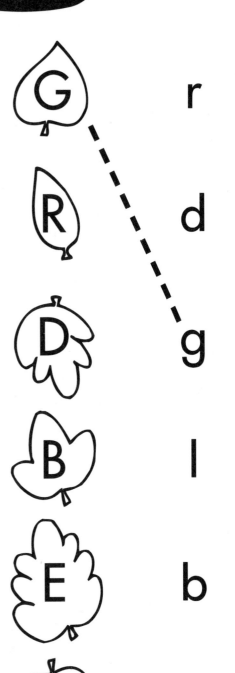

G   r

R   d

D   g

B   l

E   b

L   e

A   i

F   a

I   q

Q   w

M   f

W   m

0-7682-2920-0 *Getting Ready to Teach Reading for the New Teach*

Listen and Trace

Directions: Say the name of each picture. Trace the letter that makes the **beginning** sound.

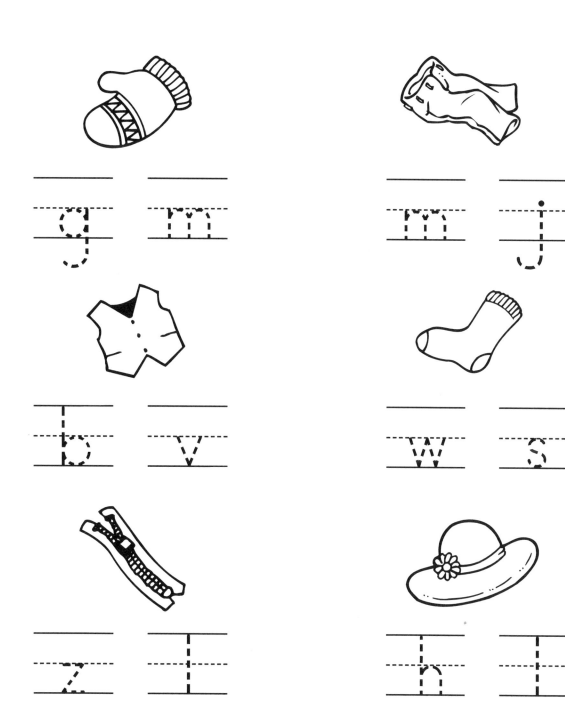

© McGraw-Hill Children's Publishing
0-7682-2920-0 *Getting Ready to Teach Reading for the New Teacher*

Food Fun

Directions: Look at the pictures in each row. Color the picture with the same **beginning** sound as the first picture.

0-7682-2920-0 *Getting Ready to Teach Reading for the New Teache*

The Tail End

Directions: Say the name of each pet. Write the ending sound.

(bird) ___ ___	(cat) ___ ___
(dog) ___ ___	(rabbit) ___ ___
(fish) ___ ___	(mouse) ___ ___

© McGraw-Hill Children's Publishing   0-7682-2920-0 *Getting Ready to Teach Reading for the New Teacher*

Look Inside

Directions: Read the two words on each animal. If they have the same **ending** sound, color the animal brown. If they have the same **beginning** sound, color the animal red.

bat
bad

man
pan

big
bed

dig
sag

bark
pack

go
get

cat
call

pig
bag

0-7682-2920-0 *Getting Ready to Teach Reading for the New Teache*

My Hand

Directions: Color the pictures that rhyme with the word **hand**.

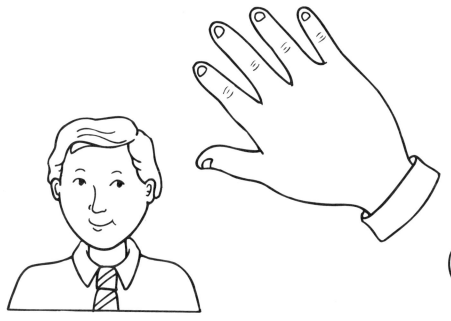

McGraw-Hill Children's Publishing

0-7682-2920-0 *Getting Ready to Teach Reading for the New Teacher*

This Is My Room

Directions: Look at this picture of my room. Circle five things that rhyme with the word **sell**.

    0-7682-2920-0 *Getting Ready to Teach Reading for the New Teacher*

Broken Hearts

Directions: Color the circle the correct color. Cut out hearts on the lines. Mix up the hearts. Can you find each match?

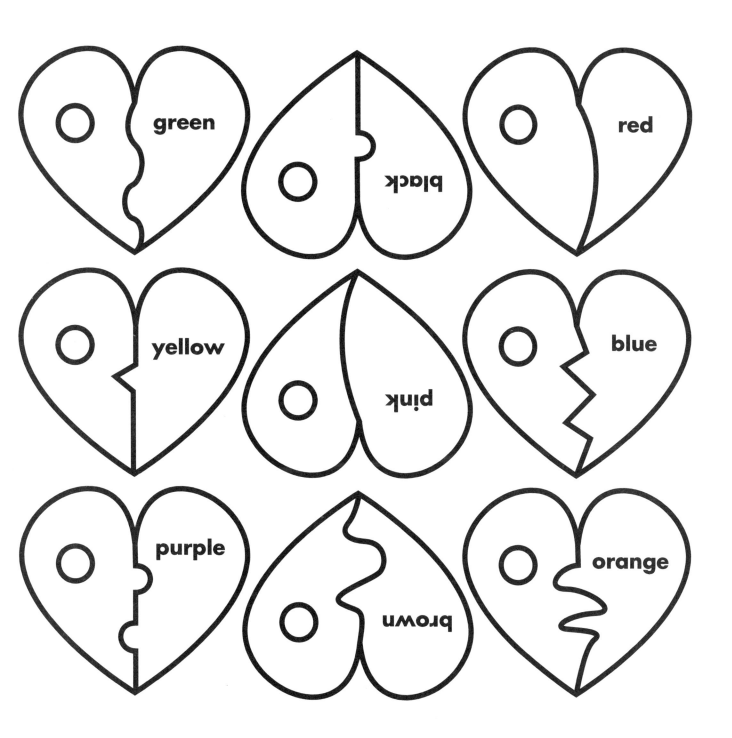

0-7682-2920-0 *Getting Ready to Teach Reading for the New Teacher*

Number, Please

Directions: Trace over the number. Cut on solid lines. Fold the number back. Read the word. Fold up flap to check.

one	1	two	2
three	3	four	4
five	5	six	6
seven	7	eight	8
nine	9	ten	10

© McGraw-Hill Children's Publishing

0-7682-2920-0 *Getting Ready to Teach Reading for the New Teacher*

The an Family—Front

Directions: Cut on solid lines. Fold on dotted lines. Fold the flaps to make words. Use the pictures to check.

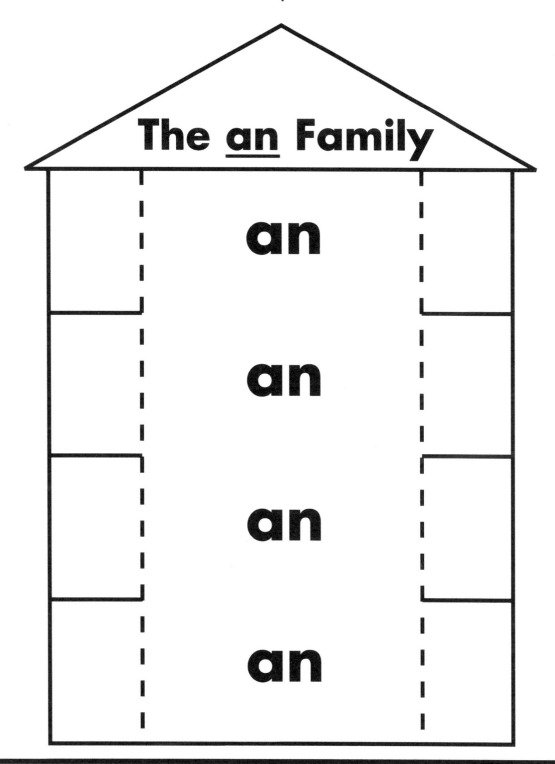

The an Family

an

an

an

an

© McGraw-Hill Children's Publishing   0-7682-2920-0 *Getting Ready to Teach Reading for the New Teacher*

The an Family—Back

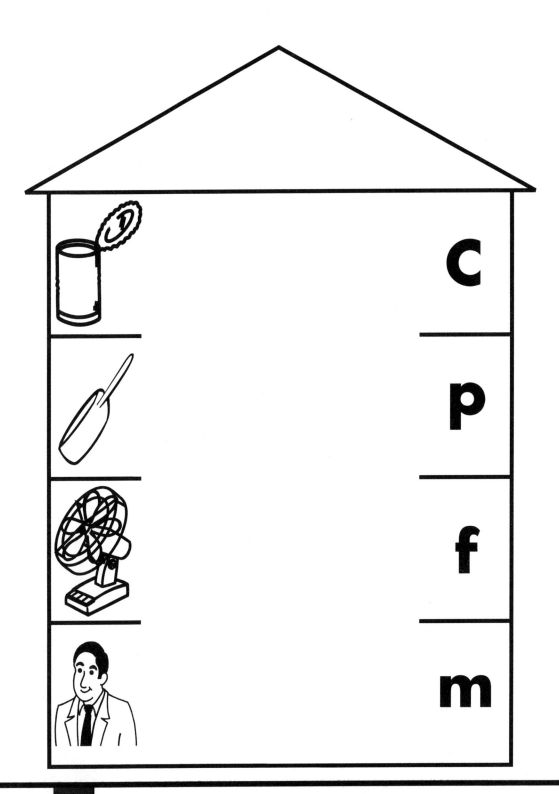

© McGraw-Hill Children's Publishing   0-7682-2920-0 *Getting Ready to Teach Reading for the New Teache*

Name _____ Date _____

What Do You See?

Directions: Cut out each strip of words below. You can put them in a pocket chart or make a mini-book. Use them to practice the sight word **the**.

I see the

I see the

I see the

I see the

0-7682-2920-0 *Getting Ready to Teach Reading for the New Teacher*

A a

apple

B b

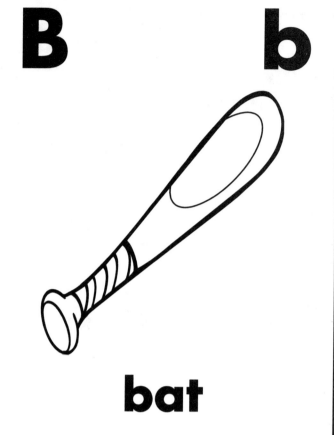

bat

C c

carrot

D d

dog

E e

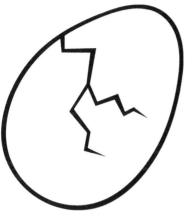

egg

F f

frog

G g

glass

H h

hand

I i

igloo

J j

jump rope

K k

king

L l

lamp

M m

milk

N n

nest

O o

octopus

P p

pan

Q q

queen

R r

ring

S s

sun

T t

tent

U u

umbrella

V v

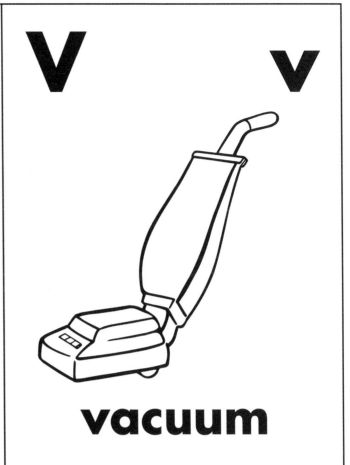

vacuum

W w

watch

X x

X-ray

Y y

yell

Z z

zipper

I KNOW MY ALPHABET LETTERS

ABCDEFGHIJKLMNOPQRSTUVWXYZ

NAME _____ DATE _____

Children's Books (mentioned in text)

Because of the wide variety of editions available, publishers and dates are not given for the children's books below. The title and author should be sufficient to find these books in the library or on the Internet. For a complete listing of alphabet books (divided by letter), see pages 140–144.

Balestrino, Philip. *The Skeleton Inside You.*

Balian, Lorna. *A Garden for a Groundhog.*

Brown, Margaret Wise. *The Noisy Book* and *The Quiet Noisy Book.*

Carle, Eric. *The Very Quiet Cricket.*

Gibbons, Gail. *The Seasons of Arnold's Apple Tree.*

Hallinan, P. K. *A Rainbow of Friends.*

Lionni, Leo. *Inch by Inch.*

Martin, Bill. *Brown Bear, Brown Bear, What Do You See?*

Marzolla, Jean. *I Spy* series.

McKee, David. *Elmer* series.

Salisbury, Kent. *A Bear Ate My Pear* (POP into Phonics books). Also, *My Nose Is a Hose* and *There's Dragon in My Wagon.*

Seuss, Dr. *Yertle the Turtle.*

Steiner, Joan. *Look-Alikes* and *Look-Alikes, Jr.*

Chapter Books (mentioned in text)

The following two series are great for read-aloud time. The chapters are short and kindergartners love the stories!

Hurwitz, Johanna. *Rip-Roaring Russell, Russell Sprouts, Russell Rides Away, E is For Elisa, Russell and Elisa, Elisa in the Middle.*

Gannet, Ruth Stiles. *My Father's Dragon, Elmer and the Dragon, The Dragons of Blueland.*

McGraw-Hill Children's Publishing

0-7682-2920-0 *Getting Ready to Teach Reading for the New Teacher*

Professional Reading (for next summer!!!)

Crofton, Linda. *Dancing with the Pen: The Learner as a Writer.*

Jager Adams, Marilyn. *Phonemic Awareness in Young Children: A Classroom Curriculum.*

Mooney, Margaret E. *Reading for Life: The Learner as a Reader.*

Owocki, Gretchen. *Make Way For Literacy! Teaching the Way Young Children Learn.*

Schickedanz, Judith A. *Much More Than the ABC's: The Early Stages of Reading and Writing.*

Trelease, Jim. *The Read Aloud Handbook, 5th edition.*

To Save You Time

Many of the following books have blackline masters that can be used to make individual mini-books for the children to use. You can easily adapt them to make your own big books (by enlarging pages on the copier). Others give you easy ways to make review activities for letters and sounds.

"Black Inventors," a booklet. *Worksheet Magazine.* (Now called *Schooldays.*)

Totline "Take Home" Books. *Object Rhymes, Alphabet and Number Rhymes.*

Scholastic Books:
  Turn-to-Learn Word Family Wheels
  Turn-to-Learn Alphabet Wheels
  25 Emergent Mini-Books
  24 Holiday and Seasonal Emergent Mini-Books
  Fun Phonics Manipulatives
  30 Collaborative Books for Your Class to Make and Share, K–2

The Education Center. *I Can Make It, I Can Learn It!*

0-7682-2920-0 *Getting Ready to Teach Reading for the New Teach*

Game

Go Fish (*Alphabet*). School Zone Publishing Co. (www.schoolzone.com).

Phonemic Awareness Activities

Alphatales Learning Library. Scholastic.

Jordano, Kimberly and Kristine Johnson. *Phonemic Awareness Songs & Rhymes.*

Learning Workshop—www.learningworkshop.com.

Wright Group Big Books

Munch, Munch, Munch	*Gravity*
Mrs. Wishy Washy	*Farm Concert*
Wishy Washy Day	*Rhyming Around the Alphabet*
Little Yellow Chick	*Gravity*
Sing a Song	

Other Big Books

Berger, Melvin. *An Apple a Day* and *A Butterfly is Born.*

Cowley, Joy. *The King's Pudding.*

Gold, Kari. *A World of Homes.*

Walker, Marion. *Six Big Apples.*

CDs (also available in cassettes)

The following CDs by Jean Feldman are highly recommended. Available through Crystal Springs Books. www.crystalsprings.com. *Keep on Singing and Dancing with Dr. Jean, Dr. Jean Sings Silly Songs, Dr. Jean and Friends.*

Sing to Learn. Check out the "Phon-ercize" and "Alpha-hardy" songs.

Another great CD is available from local bookstores.

A to Z, The Animals & Me.

Alphabet Books

Because of the variety of editions available, only author and title are given for alphabet books listed below.

ENTIRE ALPHABET

Berg, Cami. *D Is for Dolphin.*

Bruchner, Susan and Linda Kingman. *Easy Phonics Readers.*

Cushman, Doug. *The ABC Mystery.*

Dandved, Kjell B. *The Butterfly Alphabet.*

Dodson, Peter. *An Alphabet of Dinosaurs.*

Ernst, Lisa Campbell. *The Letters Are Lost.*

Garten, Muriel. *The Alphabet Tale.*

Hague, Kathleen. *Alphabears.*

Johnson, Stephen T. *Alphabet City.*

Lear, Edward. *A Was Once an Apple Pie.*

Lindbergh, Reeve. *The Awful Aardvarks Go to School.*

Lionni, Leo. *The Alphabet Tree.*

Musgrove, Margaret. *Ashanti to Zulu.*

Pallotta, Jerry. *The Ocean Alphabet Book.*

Paul, Ann Whitford. *Everything to Spend the Night.*

Rankin, Laura. *The Handmade Alphabet.*

Seuss, Dr. *Dr. Seuss's ABC.*

Slate, Joseph. *Miss Bindergarten Gets Ready for Kindergarten.*

LETTER A

Arnosky, Jim. *All About Alligators.*

Bernal, Richard. *The Ants Go Marching One by One.*

Carle, Eric. *My Apron.*

Cuyler, Margery. *Ah-choo!*

Komaiko, Leah. *Annie Bananie.*

LETTER B

Cristaldi, Kathryn. *Baseball Ballerina.*

Dabcovich, Lydia. *Busy Beavers.*

Mayer, Mercer. *Bubble, Bubble.*

Orgel, Doris. *Button Soup.*

Sadler, Marilyn. *It's Not Easy Being a Bunny.*

LETTER C

Charles, Oz. *How Is a Crayon Made?*

DeRolf, Shane. *The Crayon Box That Talked.*

Kent, Jack. *The Fat Cat.*

Sierra, Judy. *Counting Crocodiles.*

Ward, Cindy. *Cookie's Week.*

LETTER D

Freymann, Saxton. *Dog Food.*

Gomi, Taro. *The Crocodile and the Dentist.*

Hall, Donald. *I Am the Dog, I Am the Cat.*

Hooks, William H. *A Dozen Dizzy Dogs.*

Pilkey, Dav. *Dog Breath.*

0-7682-2920-0 *Getting Ready to Teach Reading for the New Teach*

LETTER E

Bodeen, Stephanie. *Elizabeti's Doll.*

Calmenson, Stephanie. *Engine, Engine, Number Nine.*

Gwynne, Fred. *Easy to See Why.*

McKee, David. *Elmer.*

Ross, Tom. *Eggbert: The Slightly Cracked Egg.*

LETTER F

Brown, Margaret Wise. *Four Fur Feet.*

Ehlert, Lois. *Feathers for Lunch.*

Lionni, Leo. *Fish is Fish.*

London, Jonathan. *Froggy's First Kiss.*

McCracken, Robert. *Little Fish.*

LETTER G

Eastman, P. D. *Go, Dog, Go!*

Petach, Heidi. *Goldilocks and the Three Hares.*

Rathman, Peggy. *Good Night, Gorilla.*

Schmidt, Karen. *The Gingerbread Man.*

Sharmat, Mitchell. *Gregory, The Terrible Eater.*

LETTER H

Brett, Jan. *The Hat.*

Dorros, Arthur. *This Is My House.*

Green, Norma. *The Hole in the Dike.*

Martin, Bill. *The Happy Hippopotami.*

Slepian, Jan and Ann Seidler. *The Hungry Thing.*

LETTER I

Brown, Margaret Wise. *The Important Book.*

Buehner, Caralyn. *I Did It, I'm Sorry; It's a Spoon, Not a Shovel.*

Pallotta, Jerry. *The Icky Bug Counting Book.*

Pinczes, Elinor. *Inchworm and a Half.*

LETTER J

Adler, David A. *A Picture Book of Jesse Owens.*

Appelt, Kathi. *Bat Jamboree.*

Degen, Bruce. *Jamboree.*

Havil, Juanita. *Jamaica's Find.*

Mayer, Mercer. *Just Go to Bed.*

LETTER K

Cherry, Lynne. *The Great Kapok Tree.*

Clark, Emma C. *I Love You, Blue Kangaroo!*

Fox, Mem. *Koala Lou.*

Gelman, Rita. *A Koala Grows Up.*

Patterson, Dr. Francine. *Koko's Kitten.*

LETTER L

Carle, Eric. *The Grouchy Ladybug; The Very Lonely Firefly.*

Hoban, Tana. *Look! Look! Look!*

Schreiber, Anne. *Log Hotel.*

Waber, Bernard. *Lyle, Lyle, Crocodile.*

McGraw-Hill Children's Publishing   0-7682-2920-0 *Getting Ready to Teach Reading for the New Teacher*

LETTER M

Fincler, Judy. *Miss Malarkey Doesn't Live in Room 10.*

Franco, Betsy. *Messy Meals.*

Kraus, Robert. *Mert the Bluer; Milton the Early Riser.*

Pfister, Marcus. *Milo and the Magical Stones.*

LETTER N

Blonder, Ellen. *Noisy Breakfast.*

Freeman, Don. *Norman the Doorman.*

Gliori, Debi. *No Matter What.*

Kraus, Robert. *Noel the Coward.*

Wells, Rosemary. *Noisy Nora.*

LETTER O

Adams, Pam. *This Old Man.*

Boy, Doe. *Otter on His Own.*

Brown, Marcia. *Once a Mouse.*

Kottke, Jan. *From Acorn to Oak Tree.*

Porter, Sue. *One Potato.*

LETTER P

Calmenson, Stephanie. *The Principal's New Clothes.*

Carle, Eric. *Pancakes, Pancakes!*

Dubowski, Cathy East and Mark Dubowski. *Picky Nicky.*

Martin, Bill. *Polar Bear, Polar Bear, What Do You Hear?*

Pelham, David. *Sam's Pizza.*

LETTER Q

Brumbeau, Jeff. *The Quiltmaker's Gift.*

Carle, Eric. *The Very Quiet Cricket.*

Johnston, Tony and Tomi De Paola. *The Quilt Story.*

Polacco, Patricia. *The Keeping Quilt.*

Wood, Audrey. *Quiet as a Cricket.*

LETTER R

Christian, Peggy. *If You Find a Rock.*

Glen, Maggie. *Ruby.*

McCourt, Lisa. *The Rain Forest Counts.*

Moore, Lilian. *Little Raccoon and the Things in the Pool.*

Munsch, Robert. *Ribbon Rescue.*

LETTER S

Brown, Marcia. *Stone Soup.*

Charles, Faustin. *The Selfish Crocodile.*

Edwards, Pamela D. *Some Smug Slug.*

Murphy, Stuart J. *A Pair of Socks.*

Pelham, David. *Sam's Sandwich.*

Tolhurst, Marilyn. *Somebody and the Three Blairs.*

LETTER T

Canizares, Susan. *Two Can Do It!*

Fox, Mem. *Tough Boris.*

Gibbons, Gail. *Trains.*

Munsch, Robert. *Thomas' Snowsuit.*

Ziefert, Harriet. *When the TV Broke.*

0-7682-2920-0 *Getting Ready to Teach Reading for the New Teach*

LETTER U

Arnold, Tedd. *Five Ugly Monsters.*

Monsell, May E. *Underwear!*

Packard, Mary. *The World Up Close.*

Pinkney, Jerry. *The Ugly Duckling.*

Seuss, Dr. *Great Day for Up.*

LETTER V

Blos, Joan W. *One Very Best Valentine's Day.*

Kraus, Robert. *How Spider Saved Valentine's Day; Phil the Ventriloquist.*

Marzollo, Jean. *Valentine Cats.*

Williams, Margery. *The Velveteen Rabbit.*

LETTER W

Allard, Harry. *It's So Nice to Have a Wolf Around the House.*

Cebulash, Mel. *Willie's Wonderful Pet.*

Glaser, Linda. *Wonderful Worms.*

LeSieg, Theo. *Wacky Wednesday.*

Peet, Bill. *The Wump World.*

LETTER X

Balestrino, Philip. *The Skeleton Inside You.* (X-ray)

LETTER Y

Martel, Cruz. *Yagua Days.*

LETTER Z

Campbell, Rod. *Dear Zoo.*

Fox, Mem. *Zoo-Looking.*

Moss, Lloyd. *Zin! Zin! A Violin.*

Paxton, Tom. *Going to the Zoo.*

Pulver, Robin. *Mrs. Toggle's Zipper.*

McGraw-Hill Children's Publishing

0-7682-2920-0 *Getting Ready to Teach Reading for the New Teacher*

Web Site List

▶ International Reading Association (IRA)
www.reading.org

▶ National Association for the Education of Young Children (NAEYC)
www.naeyc.org

▶ No Child Left Behind Legislation
www.nclb.gov

▶ "Put Reading First" Document
http://www.nifl.gov/partnershipforreading/publications/reading_first1.html

▶ Align to Achieve State Standard Database (standards by state, grade level, subject)
www.aligntoachieve.org

▶ State Standard Correlations (McGraw-Hill Children's Publishing products)
www.MHstandards.com

0-7682-2920-0 *Getting Ready to Teach Reading for the New Teacher*